DO-IT-YOURSELF GUIDES

Essential Auto Maintenance

Quality tools to build your world.

ACKNOWLEDGEMENTS

Created by Creative Publishing international
in conjunction with WSP Marketing International Ltd.,
47 Valleybrook Drive, Don Mills, Ontario M3B 2S6,
Canada.

**Creative Publishing international
Book Development Staff**

Vikki Anderson
Shawn Binkowski
Steve Boman
Janice Cauley
Marcia Chambers
Maren Christensen
Paul Currie
Doug Deutscher
Melissa Erickson
Jacque Fletcher
John Fletcher
Brad Kissell
Janet Lawrence
Bill Nelson
Chuck Nields
Jon Simpson
Greg Wallace
Gina Wornson

Printed on Canadian paper by World Color
Book Services, USA.

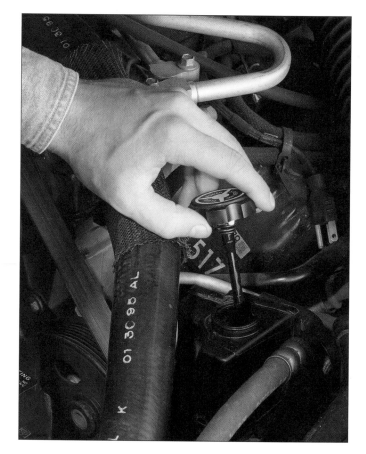

ISBN 0-86573-763-0

This book provides useful instructions but
we cannot anticipate all of your working
conditions or the characteristics of your
materials and tools. For safety, you should
use caution, care and good judgement
when following the procedures described in
this book. Consider your own skill level and
the instructions and safety precautions
associated with the various tools and
materials shown.

Creative Publishing international, WSP
Marketing International Ltd., Canadian Tire
Corporation, Ltd., or the Canadian Tire
Associate Dealers do not assume any
responsibility for damage to property
or injury to persons as a result of the use
of the information contained in this book.

Before commencing any project, consult
your local Building Department for information on building permits, codes and other
laws, as they may apply to your project.

INTRODUCTION

Keeping your vehicle on the road safely, dependably and economically can be a daily challenge. There are so many things you need to know, sometimes just understanding what to do can be a problem. *Essential Auto Maintenance* provides the solution with practical information and step-by-step maintenance and repair projects to keep your vehicle running well – and to troubleshoot when things go wrong.

Essential Auto Maintenance is divided into sections covering your vehicle's major systems. Detailed instructions and full-colour photographs guide you through all of the basic maintenance and repairs your vehicle needs. You'll see how to set up a functional work area where you can properly store the Mastercraft tools you need to keep your vehicle in great shape. There are projects for installing practical accessories and for simple body repairs. You'll find an overview of how to prepare your vehicle for the rigours of summer or winter driving, and information covering roadside emergencies. You'll even find a troubleshooting section with tips for identifying problems such as troublesome noises, or why your vehicle won't start – and what you can do about it.

Essential Auto Maintenance will help put you in control of your vehicle – and save you money, too. Welcome to the world of Mastercraft Do-It-Yourself Guides!

TABLE OF CONTENTS

Garage Workshop Setup 6

Automotive Systems Overview 12

Maintenance Tips & Techniques 16

Auto Body Care & Repair 48

Installing Accessories 52

Troubleshooting 56

Index 62

Having the right tools at hand is essential to doing any kind of maintenance or repair properly and quickly. Trying to make do with the wrong or poor quality tools will lead to frustration and damaged parts. The tools shown here will allow you to do the projects in this book. You do not need to purchase everything at one time, but can build up your collection as each project requires.

Since most of the work you will do will be on your vehicle, having a sheltered

work area (like a garage) large enough to hold your vehicle while giving you enough room to comfortably move around it is ideal, particularly if the garage is heated. Of course, you can always work outdoors if the weather is cooperative. Other than adequate tool storage facilities, all you will probably need for additional workspace is a small but sturdy workbench (2x4' is a good size). Attaching a small metal vise to it will be useful.

Basic tools: *garden hose with sprayer (A), rubber gloves (B), worklight (C), ratchet and socket set (D), spatula (E), baster (F), scrub brush (G), screwdriver set (H), wrench set (I), torque wrenches (J), windshield squeegee (K), fire extinguisher (L), wire cutter/stripper (M), small wire brush (N), artist brushes (O), eye goggles (P), slip/combination pliers (Q), Robo-Grip® pliers (R), prybar (S).*

Specialty repair tools: battery charger (A), spark plug sockets (B), oil filter wrench (C), antifreeze hydrometer (D), battery fluid hydrometer (E), jumper cables (F), fuse puller (G), battery cable puller (H), feeler gauge set (I), plastic body filler applicator (J), suction-cup dent puller (K), slide-hammer dent puller (L).

Auto shop accessories: ramps (A), stool (B), creeper (C), axle/jack stands (D), hydraulic trolley jack (E), oil catch basin (F), landscaping drain pipe (G), wheel chocks (H), tow strap (I).

Power tools: palm sander (A), heat gun (B), cordless drill (C), drill bits, including screwdriver bit (D).

Working Safely:

- When working underneath a vehicle never rely on a jack of any kind to support the vehicle. The jack is to simply raise and lower the vehicle. Use axle/jack stands or ramps to actually support the vehicle. They are inexpensive and well worth the few dollars' investment.

- Use wheel chocks of some kind (large bricks work well) on any wheels on the ground.

- Drive-up ramps are an option for safely working under the vehicle if you will not be doing any wheel or suspension work. Have a helper guide you up the ramps.

- Work on level ground, leaving an automatic transmission in Park and a manual transmission in first gear. Apply the parking brake as well.

- Remove watch, rings and any other jewellery. Also make sure you do not have any loose clothing or dangling hair that can get caught by a spinning fan belt.

- Never run the engine in an enclosed space, unless you first attach a large-diameter hose to the exhaust pipe to direct the exhaust outdoors. Plastic landscaping drain pipe works well for this – get the version with no holes in it. Install a carbon monoxide (CO) alarm for added safety.

- Wear safety glasses or goggles, especially if you will be under the vehicle.

- Be comfortable. If you will be working under the car, buy a creeper so you can move around easily. Or if you will be working stooped over, use a small stool or

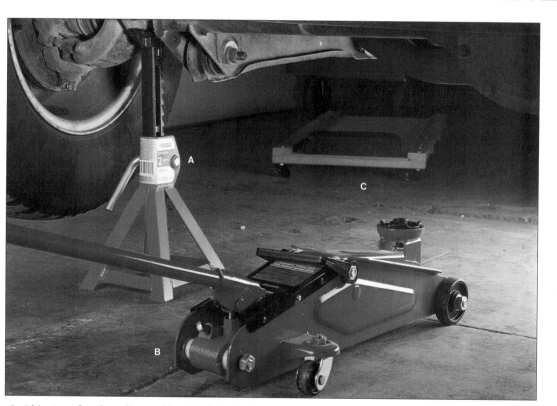

A 1¹/₂-ton hydraulic trolley jack (B) should handle all your needs in your garage workshop. Use the jack to raise your vehicle enough to place 2-ton axle/jack stands (A) in position to support the vehicle. Never work on your vehicle when it is supported only by a jack. A creeper (C) makes it much easier to work underneath the vehicle.

Never run your vehicle *in a closed workshop without a means to vent the exhaust fumes outside. Use a piece of landscaping drain pipe that is long enough to be placed over the exhaust pipe and then routed to the outdoors.*

TIPS:

Always keep a roll of paper towel and glass cleaner near your workbench. This way you will always have clean safety glasses to wear while working on your projects.

❖❖❖❖❖❖❖❖❖❖❖❖

Disposable surgical-style rubber gloves are very useful for auto work. They protect your hands while allowing you to feel what you are doing because of their thin material. They are inexpensive and can be purchased in bulk quantities.

one of the rolling stools available. Both will save your back and keep you from getting too tired to work safely.

❑ Have enough light to see what you are doing.

❑ No smoking or open flames. Gasoline fumes are explosive.

❑ Have a fire extinguisher in the shop, and check it yearly to make sure it is properly charged.

❑ If working alone, have someone check on you every so often.

❑ Read the labels of the products used for auto care. Be extra careful with those that warn against breathing fumes or skin contact, and make sure there is adequate ventilation in your work area.

❑ Old engine oil is filled with toxic compounds. Avoid handling it as much as possible. Wear rubber gloves.

❑ Work on a cool engine whenever possible. Be aware that electric fans can switch on without the engine running.

❑ Do not work on a car when you are tired or have been drinking.

A worklight is very helpful, *even in a well-lighted workshop. There are often areas, such as under the hood or underneath the chassis, where you need a portable light source so you can work efficiently and safely.*

Mastercraft Essential Auto Maintenance

Tool Storage

A toolbox should be considered another tool that helps you get the job done. You can save yourself a lot of time and frustration with a little organization. It can be very frustrating to be knee-deep in a repair, need a specific tool and not be able to locate it. It can turn a quick and simple repair into an all-day scavenger hunt.

You do not have to spend a lot of money to organize your tool collection. Even the most basic tool chest, plus a few additional organizers, will help. Buy a toolbox that will help you organize (photo above). The more drawers or trays it has, the easier it is to sort tools into categories and applications. Have one drawer reserved for special tools that you use rarely; another for sockets and ratchet handles, and so on. It will not take long to fill up any extra space. If you have a lot of tools and consistently work in the same space, a large stacking tool chest, with multiple levels and drawers, on a roller cabinet is the best (photo right). While initially more expensive, it will last a lifetime. Stacking tool chests allow you to customize your storage needs,

allowing you to add additional units as need demands.

If you do not have a garage, or a very large collection of tools, a smaller metal or plastic toolbox is the best alternative. Even if you have a large stacking tool chest, you should have a portable box as well, so you may take tools to any repair location. Plastic boxes are lighter, but offer few drawers. Metal toolboxes are generally sturdier, can be found with a variety of drawer configurations, but are heavier and usually more expensive.

When putting tools into a stacking tool chest and cabinet, put the heaviest but least-used items in the lower drawers. This also keeps the tool chest properly balanced. Save the upper drawers for the items you will be reaching for the most, like sockets, screwdrivers, pliers and wrenches.

Tool Storage Ideas:

❑ Whatever kind of toolbox or tool chest you choose, line the shelves or drawers with some type of protective padding (photo below). This helps keep tools in place and prevents damage to them and to the toolbox.

❑ In addition, protect your expensive tools and toolboxes from rust. Place inexpensive rust-preventing paper or other products that absorb water vapour in the drawers (photo below). These products are available at hardware and auto parts stores.

❑ The best ways to store sockets are either on spring-loaded clips or in magnetic socket holders.

❑ Do not store parts, supplies and fasteners in the toolbox. Instead, separate them into plastic storage units with multiple bins. This will allow for quick access and lower the risk of damage to the parts.

❑ Hanging tools on a wall-mounted rack or peg-board can be great, but can often cost much more than a good toolbox.

❑ Kitchen cabinets, perhaps salvaged from a remodelling project, are excellent for storing larger items and supplies. You can purchase inexpensive unfinished cabinets new and use them as a base for a workbench. Wall cabinets provide a safe place for supplies and tools that you want out of the reach of children.

❑ While you can buy some tool sets complete with a toolbox, decide if you are really getting what you need. Do not purchase a tool set just because the toolbox is included, or vice versa.

TIPS:

Use the upper drawers of your toolbox for your Mastercraft sockets, screwdrivers, pliers and wrenches for effective organization that will simplify your repair project.

❖❖❖❖❖❖❖❖❖❖❖❖❖❖❖❖❖❖❖❖❖❖❖❖❖

Whether you choose a rugged Mastercraft toolbox or a Mastercraft tool chest and cabinet, make sure to buy more toolbox than you need. This makes expansion of your tool collection easy.

Toolboxes and stacking tool chest/cabinets *not only organize your tools, they protect them as well. Wrench organizer strips (A) and drawer dividers (B) help provide best use of storage space. Drawers lined with a protective padding (C) and containing a rust prevention product (D) will help your valuable tools provide years of service.*

Good mechanics spend time in classes and make the effort to stay current with changes in technology. Consider taking a course in automotive technology at a local school or college. Once you understand the theories behind how a car starts, goes, stops, turns and deals with the weather, you will be well prepared to make automotive repairs. Before making any major repairs, purchase a good quality repair manual written for your vehicle's make and year. Get to know the people behind the parts counter at your auto centre. Often they know about the ins and outs of a specific repair, and will steer you around the not-so-obvious difficulties.

Keep in mind that an engine needs three things in order to run: fuel, air and a spark (electricity) to ignite the fuel/air mixture. When you are faced with an engine that will not start or run properly, determine what needs repair by analyzing those three basic things. Is it getting enough fuel, at the right time? Is the flow of air to the engine unimpeded? Finally, is electricity getting to the motor and the ignition system at the right time? What you find out by answering those three questions determines what you do next.

Where & What Things Are

Today's cars and trucks have thousands of parts, each with a specific job to do. Here are common parts you should know about, plus a brief explanation of their function. The illustrations on pages 12–15 show typical locations for many of these parts. **NOTE:** Consult your owner's manual to find specific details relating to your vehicle's major systems.

Under the Hood:

❏ Air cleaner: Houses the air filter, which cleans the air brought into the engine cylinders.

❏ Alternator: Generator that produces alternating current (AC) to keep the electrical system and battery charged.

❏ Brake booster: Device operated by either vacuum/air pressure or power steering pressure to reduce braking effort.

❏ Carburetor or fuel injection system: Mixes fuel and air and delivers the mixture to the engine's combustion chamber.

❏ Charcoal canister filter: Stores fuel vapours and returns them to fuel tank.

❏ Coolant recovery bottle: Stores and returns coolant to the radiator after the engine cools.

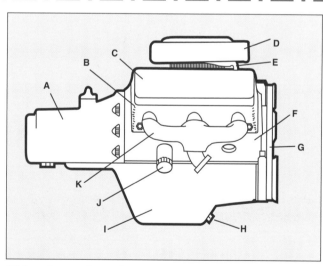

Side view of engine: *transmission (A), cylinder head (B), valve cover (C), air cleaner (D), carburetor (E), cylinder block (F), serpentine belt/drive belt (G), oil pan plug (H), oil pan (I), oil filter (J), exhaust manifold (K), as shown on a carbureted engine.*

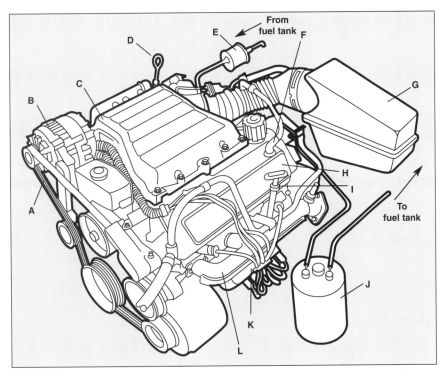

Top ¾ view of engine: serpentine belt/drive belt (A), alternator (B), intake manifold (C), oil dipstick (D), fuel filter (E), PCV valve (F), air cleaner (G), valve cover (H), transmission dipstick (I), charcoal canister filter (J), distributor (K), exhaust manifold (L), as shown on a fuel-injected engine.

❏ **Coolant sensor:** Measures engine coolant temperature.

❏ **Crank sensor/cam sensor:** Sensors that provide the engine computer with information necessary to set engine timing and injector fuel delivery.

❏ **Cylinder block:** Houses all major mechanical engine parts; filled with passages for lubricants and coolant.

❏ **Cylinder head:** Contains the intake and exhaust valves, and passageways that allow the air/fuel mixture to enter (intake) and exhaust fumes to leave (exhaust) the cylinders.

❏ **Distributor:** Transfers the voltage surge from the ignition coil to the spark plugs via the distributor cap and high energy spark plug wires in the correct firing order.

❏ **ECU (electronic control unit, but also called an ECM or PCM):** The engine computer. By looking at information from various sensors, makes adjustments to operate the engine at optimum settings.

❏ **Exhaust manifold:** Tubes that direct exhaust gases away from the engine.

❏ **Firewall:** The body piece between the engine compartment and the passenger compartment.

❏ **Fuel filter:** Catches and removes particles from fuel coming from the fuel tank.

❏ **Fuel injector:** Electrically controlled solenoid valve that delivers a controlled amount of pressurized fuel into the combustion chamber.

❏ **Fuel pressure regulator:** Maintains proper fuel pressure.

❏ **Idle air control (IAC):** Regulates idle speed in fuel-injected engines.

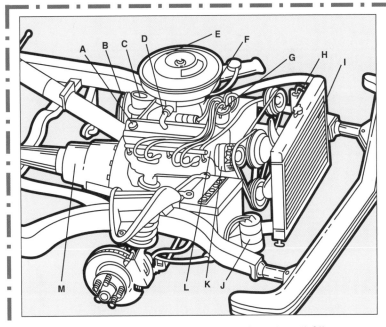

Side ¾ view of engine and front chassis: oil filler cap (A), brake booster (B), master cylinder (C), PCV valve (D), air cleaner (E), intake manifold (F), distributor (G), coolant recovery bottle (H), radiator (I), charcoal canister filter (J), alternator (K), cylinder head (L), transmission (M), as shown on a carbureted engine.

- Intake manifold: Directs the fuel/air mixture into the cylinders.

- Master cylinder: Creates the hydraulic pressure for the brake system and stores brake fluid.

- Oil filler cap: Location where motor oil is added.

- Oil filter: Catches and removes particles from the motor oil.

- Oxygen (O_2) sensor: Measures the amount of oxygen in the exhaust; sends a signal to the engine computer to adjust the air/fuel mixture.

- Park/Neutral (PRNDL), reverse lamp switch: Switch that turns on the back-up lights when the vehicle is in reverse and tells the engine computer in which gear the transmission selector has been placed. Keeps the engine from being started in any gear except Park or Neutral.

- PCV (positive crankcase ventilation) valve: Emission device that routes crankcase vapours to the intake manifold to be burned during combustion.

- Power steering reservoir: Holds fluid used to create hydraulic pressure for steering system.

- Radiator: The heart of the cooling system, it provides a way for the engine to discharge the heat that is produced by combustion.

- Radiator hoses/heater hoses: Carry coolant between the engine block, heater core and radiator.

- Serpentine belt/drive belt: Drives the water pump, power steering pump, emission air pump and air conditioning compressor.

- Throttle position sensor (TPS): Monitors the position of the throttle.

- Transmission dipstick and tube: Where to check and add automatic transmission fluid.

- Water pump: Part of the cooling system that circulates the coolant through the block, radiator and heater core.

Front Undercarriage:

- Drive axle: Transfers energy from the transaxle or transmission to the wheels.

- Petcock: Small valve, either metal or plastic, at the bottom of the radiator for draining coolant.

- Rack and pinion steering gear: Type of steering assembly connected to the steering wheel.

- Transaxle: Combination transmission (manual or automatic) and differential unit used in front wheel drive cars.

- Transmission: A housing containing a series of gears that converts the engine's power into movement.

Rear Undercarriage:

- Catalytic converter: Part of the exhaust system that reduces harmful emissions.

- Differential: Gear assembly on rear wheel drive cars used to transfer power from the transmission and drive shaft to the rear wheels.

- Fuel tank: Stores gasoline or diesel fuel and their vapours.

- Muffler: Reduces the noise produced by an internal combustion engine.

- Shock absorbers: Use air or hydraulic pressure to smooth and reduce the up-and-down motion of a vehicle.

- Springs: Help maintain normal vehicle height.

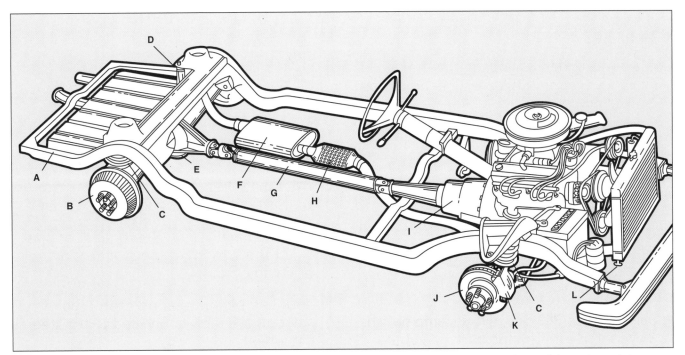

Vehicle chassis as shown on a rear wheel drive vehicle: fuel tank (A), brake drum (B), springs (C), shock absorber (D), differential (E), muffler (F), driveshaft (G), catalytic converter (H), transmission (I), brake rotor (J), disc brake caliper (K), petcock (L).

Brakes and Suspension:

❏ Brake drums: On drum brakes, the large housing that surrounds the brake shoes and provides a friction surface for the brake shoes to stop a vehicle.

❏ Brake pads: On disc brakes, the replaceable friction material that is forced against the rotor to stop a vehicle.

❏ Brake rotors: On disc brakes, the metal disc that brake pads are forced against to stop a vehicle.

❏ Brake shoes: On drum brakes, the curved replaceable friction material forced against the drum to stop a vehicle.

❏ Disc brake caliper: Assembly that holds the brake pads and wheel cylinder.

❏ Strut cartridge: Replaceable shock absorber unit of a strut system.

❏ Wheel cylinder: Hydraulic piston that pushes the brake shoes against the drums.

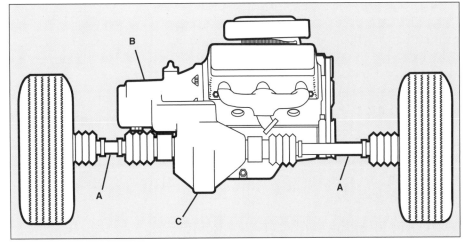

Front axle and engine for front wheel drive vehicle: drive axles (A), transmission (B), transaxle (C), as seen from the rear of the vehicle.

MAINTENANCE TIPS & TECHNIQUES

Ignoring manufacturers' maintenance schedules is the number one cause of vehicle failures. Compared to the overall cost of a new vehicle, investing a few dollars and a couple of hours a few times a year is a good tradeoff. Be sure to change your oil religiously. Not only will your engine thank you with better reliability and gas mileage, but you may also head off problems that have nothing to do with the engine. An oil change forces you under the hood, providing an opportunity to check over things and look for obvious problems.

There are few real shortcuts. Most basic maintenance jobs and repairs have a set number of steps that must be performed in the correct order. Trying to speed up by doing things out of sequence or skipping steps usually means you will run into unexpected problems. You may even find you have to start over.

Specialized tools exist for a reason. There are simply some things you cannot accomplish without the specialized tool designed for a specific task or to fit a particular part.

Do not ignore measurements. Many repairs and basic maintenance steps require that accurate measurements are taken, and adjustments made as needed. A common example is a spark plug gap. New plugs do not come gapped correctly. The plug manufacturer expects you to set them at the proper gap, which varies by engine and make. Invest in some basic but accurate measuring tools, and use them.

Reusing gaskets does not save money. If there is a gasket involved, the safe and smart course is always to replace it with a new one. Failing to do this usually means you get everything back together and after starting the engine, you now have a brand new leak to fix.

The tune-up, as we've known it, is a thing of the past. Today computers make adjustments as we drive. Depending on how long you own your car, you may never have to do a traditional tune-up. Engines now burn fuel so efficiently there is less carbon fouling on the spark plugs. Depending on the engine, it is not uncommon to expect 100,000 km (60,000 mi) out of a set of spark plugs. In place of the traditional tune-up there is a filter tune-up designed to keep all the sensors and electronics operating properly.

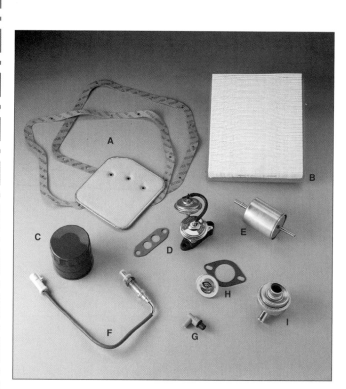

Specialty filters and valves: *transmission filter with gaskets (A), air filter (B), oil filter (C), EGR valve/filter with mounting gasket (D), fuel filter (E), O₂ sensor (F), PCV valve (G), thermostat with mounting gasket (H), transaxle filter (I).*

Fluids: antifreeze (A), windshield washer solution (B), gear oil (C), distilled water (D), white grease (E), transmission fluid (F), power steering fluid (G), brake fluid (H), motor oil (I).

Maintenance Checklist:

❑ When replacing any filter, buy the best products because these items are too important for your vehicle's health to justify saving a few dollars. When in doubt as to whether or not a filter needs replacing, replace it.

❑ Air Filters: Replace every 19,000 to 24,000 km (12,000 to 15,000 mi).

❑ Automatic Transmission/Transaxle Filter & Fluid: Change filter and fluid every 24 months or 48,000 km (30,000 mi).

❑ Brake Fluid: Flush and replace fluid every 2 years or 48,000 km (30,000 mi).

❑ Charcoal Canister Filter: Replace every 24,000 km (15,000 mi) or every tune-up. **NOTE:** Not all vehicles have this filter.

❑ Exhaust Gas Recirculation (EGR) Valve & Filter: Replace every 24,000 km (15,000 mi) or with every tune-up. **NOTE:** Not all vehicles have this filter.

❑ Fuel Filter: Replace every 19,000 to 24,000 km (12,000 to 15,000 mi) or with every tune-up.

❑ Manual Transmission Filter & Fluid: Change filter and fluid every 2 years or 48,000 km (30,000 mi). The fluid should be checked every 12,000 km (7,500 mi).

❑ Oil Changes: Every 5,000 to 8,000 km (3,000 to 5,000 mi).

❑ Oil Filter: Replace every 5,000 to 8,000 km (3,000 to 5,000 mi) when changing the oil.

❑ Oxygen (O_2) Sensor: Replace every 3 years.

❑ Positive Crankcase Ventilation (PCV) Valve & Filter: Replace every 16,000 to 24,000 km (10,000 to 15,000 mi).

❑ Thermostat: Replace every 2 years or 48,000 km (30,000 mi) as a part of the cooling system flush and refill.

- Timing Belt: As a general rule, the timing belt should be replaced during the engine's life. In a belt-driven camshaft, replace belt between 72,000 to 145,000 km (45,000 to 90,000 mi). In an overhead camshaft engine, replace belt between 64,000 to 128,000 km (40,000 to 80,000 mi). If your owner's manual carries a specific warning about the timing belt, take notice.

- Alignment/Wheel Balance: There is not a particular time you should have an alignment done or check your wheel balance. However you may need to have an alignment done on your car if you have any of the following symptoms:
  - the tires are wearing too fast and unevenly,
  - you have to make constant steering adjustments while driving down a straight road,
  - the vehicle shakes or vibrates at certain speeds or continuously,
  - it pulls to one side or another as you drive or brake.

- Wheel Balance: Check the wheel balance if the steering wheel vibrates either side-to-side or up-and-down.

- Tire Rotation: Every 10,000 km (6,000 mi) or when tires show signs of uneven wear.

- Tire Rotation Pattern: Rotating the tires to different positions on your vehicle will obtain the maximum mileage out of the tires and will keep the best tires on the front wheels for safe driving. The rotation pattern depends on the type of tires and the type of vehicle: rear wheel drive (RWD), front wheel drive (FWD), all wheel drive (AWD) or 4 wheel drive (4WD). Check for proper rotation patterns where you purchase the tires. If you have a full-size spare, it can be included as part of a five-tire rotation. However, never include a space-saver spare tire when rotating your tires. If you have a space-saver spare tire be sure to check its pressure every six months and before taking a long trip.

Transmission Service

Due to their complexity, automatic transmissions are difficult and expensive to repair. Just like the engine they are bolted to, transmissions – both manual and automatic – require periodic maintenance and proper treatment.

Transmission Maintenance Checklist:

- Check the fluid level at least once a month. Set the parking brake, place the shifter in Park, and run the car at operating temperature and on a level surface.

- If fluid needs to be added, make sure you use the correct type (see your owner's manual or talk to your dealer).

- Use overdrive when driving. Most manufacturers recommend driving in this gear, even if most of the driving you do is "city driving," to help increase fuel economy.

*Your vehicle may have a **dip-stick*** *for checking the transmission fluid level. If it does not, you will have to check the fluid level from underneath the vehicle.*

- Changing the filter and fluid every 24 months or 48,000 km (30,000 mi) is crucial for the long life of an automatic transmission. Transmission fluid helps keep the transmission cool by absorbing the tremendous heat that develops inside a transmission.

TIP:

Be sure you are at a complete stop when shifting from Reverse to Park. Never shift into gear while racing the engine. Too much strain is placed on the transmission case, internal parts and engine mounts.

Checking Transmission Fluid

Manual transmissions require fluid checks during every scheduled service, or every 12,000 km (7,500 mi). Typically, the fluid should be changed every two years or 48,000 km (30,000 mi). If you take your vehicle off-road, tow a trailer or do all city driving, it should be changed sooner. Many cars now have a dip-stick and filler tube under the hood, making it easy to check and add fluid if necessary. For other cars, the fluid must be checked from under the car.

How to Check Transmission Fluid

1 On most cars there are two plugs on the transmission case. Clean off the plug closest to the top of the car.

2 Use a wrench to remove the plug. Be careful if the fluid is hot. Let it cool before checking.

3 Stick your finger or a bent pipe cleaner into the hole. The fluid should be no more than 1/2" below the fill hole.

4 Fill to the correct level with the proper grade of lubricant, using a funnel. Never overfill the transmission, as too much fluid will cause air bubbles to form.

Testing Transmission Fluid

The following test will help you determine when it is time to change fluid regardless of mileage. Drip a few drops of the transmission fluid onto a clean, white piece of paper. Compare the spot to our list.

❏ CLEAR, pinkish red or green – colour varies by fluid type used (photo right, A): When it looks like this, it is still okay.

❏ WHITISH, or with a milk-shake look to it (photo right, B): You probably have a leak in the transmission cooler that is allowing coolant to mix with the transmission fluid. Have this fixed right away before it turns into an expensive repair.

❏ DARK REDDISH BROWN (photo right, C): If it has a burnt aroma and looks burnt, it is overdue for a change. The fluid has lost its ability to lubricate.

❏ METAL PARTICLES VISIBLE (photo right, D): This could be a sign of high wear and possible damage. Some metal debris is normal, so first get the fluid and filter changed right away. Drive a few thousand kilometres, and then have another fluid/filter change. If there is still a lot of metal debris in the fluid, take it to your dealer for an evaluation and possible repair.

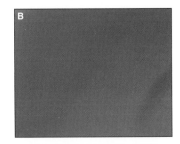

Electrical Problems

Vehicles run as much on electricity as they do on gasoline. You must have an electrical system delivering a reliable supply of energy, or your vehicle simply will not function properly and may not even start. But electrical problems are among the hardest to resolve. Often the problems occur on an irregular basis, making diagnosis and repair difficult because the conditions cannot be reliably duplicated. These intermittent electrical problems will make even the best mechanics cringe.

It helps to remember that electricity is sneaky. Electricity is always looking to complete a circuit by finding the path of least resistance. Electricity should follow the vehicle's designed system, but if there is a problem it may result in a short circuit. And when you have a short circuit, fuses blow in order to protect you and your vehicle.

Whenever the electricity quits flowing, the first place to check is the fuse panel. A modern car can have 20 or more fuses. Check your owner's manual to locate them. Sometimes temporary conditions cause a fuse to blow, so all you need to do is replace the fuse. If it continues to blow, you have a short that must be tracked down. It pays to buy a package of spare fuses and an appropriate fuse puller (photo opposite page bottom). Usually the vehicle comes with only a few spares. Never use a fuse with a different amperage than the original. Doing so may lead to damage or even a fire.

TIP:

After troubleshooting the electrical problem, always disconnect the battery (photo right) when cleaning contacts and terminals or doing extensive work on the electrical system. This will prevent injury to you as well as damage to tools or parts.

Troubleshooting Techniques:

❑ Does any light flickering problem strike most often during or just after rainy or humid spells? If so, corrosion on an electrical connection is usually the culprit. Often, simply checking, cleaning and tightening the connection solves the problem (photo opposite page top). A small wire brush (brass is best) and some spray-on contact cleaner will remove the dirt and get the electricity flowing again. Make sure the power is off when cleaning any electrical connector (photo below).

Always remove the negative battery terminal cable *before doing any electrical work. You may need to use a screwdriver to spread the cable clamp apart before you can use the terminal puller to remove the cable.*

❏ You will often find that the bulb sockets are the problem, so always clean the sockets first, before replacing the bulb. Placing a small amount of white grease on the base of the bulb will help keep it from corroding again and will make the bulb easier to remove the next time it has to be replaced.

❏ If the contacts or terminals are so badly corroded that no amount of brushing will get them clean, buy replacements at your auto centre. Also purchase quick-splice connectors necessary for an easy fix.

❏ If your electrical problems continue, consult a professional. Finding and repairing electrical shorts is a challenge. Go to a shop that specializes in electrical systems.

Use a small wire brush and contact cleaner to remove corrosion from electrical connections to ensure proper contact. Corroded connections are a frequent cause of electrical problems.

Always make sure you have replacement fuses in all the sizes your vehicle requires. Use a fuse puller (A) to remove blown fuses. You can snap in the replacement with your fingers.

MASTERCRAFT

BASIC HAND TOOLS

- terminal puller
- wire brush
- hydrometer/ battery tester
- voltmeter
- nylon scrub brush
- kitchen baster
- battery charger

NEEDED MATERIALS

- distilled water
- battery cleaner product
- toothpicks
- rubber gloves

Always purchase a battery that meets your vehicle's requirements (see your owner's manual for specifications). A quality battery will have a high reserve capacity (over 80 minutes), and cold-cranking amps (over 500).

TIP:

When disconnecting either of the battery cables for any reason, make sure the ignition key is in the "Off" position and all lights and accessories are turned off. If removing both battery cables, always disconnect the negative cable first, and reconnect it last.

Batteries

Most people do not think of the battery as something that needs attention. The reality is that all batteries, even the so-called maintenance-free types, should receive an annual check-up. The best time is probably in the fall, just before the cold weather settles in.

If you have to replace your old battery, replace it with one that has a high reserve capacity, amperage-hour rating and cold-cranking amps. Be sure that the battery you buy is the correct size for your vehicle. It must fit snugly in the battery hold-down clamps. The new battery should have the terminals in the same place as the old one. Battery cables are usually short and will not stretch to fit a terminal in a new spot. Purchase maintenance-free batteries. Check the condition of the battery hold-downs and battery cables. A cable that is falling apart or can not be adequately tightened onto the terminal should be replaced along with the battery.

How to Check a Battery

1 If you have a non-sealed battery, purchase a hydrometer/battery tester (which measures the specific gravity of the battery fluid) and use it to measure each cell of the battery. Remove the battery cap, insert the hydrometer and suction out a quantity of battery fluid. The hydrometer will indicate the level of specific gravity or charge (1.25 being a good level; see instructions supplied with the hydrometer). Write down the number you get for each individual cell. If any two cells differ in specific gravity by more than .05, you are probably going to have to replace the battery.

2 Purchase some distilled water at the grocery store and use it to slowly top off the water level in each battery cell. A kitchen baster is a good tool for this. Replace the caps. **OPTION:** If you have a maintenance-free battery, you will need a voltmeter (which measures the voltage of the battery). Attach the voltmeter leads to the battery terminals (positive lead to positive terminal, negative lead to negative terminal). The voltmeter should indicate at least 12.0 volts. If it does not, recharge the battery.

3 Clean the battery with a mixture of baking soda and water. A nylon scrub brush comes in handy, and you may need to plug any cell cap vents with toothpicks. There are also battery cleaner products available at auto parts stores.

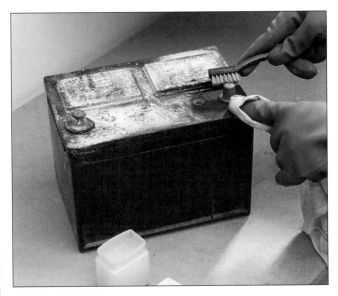

Keep battery terminals clean and free of corrosion. Use a wire brush to remove corrosion, then prevent its return with a film of petroleum jelly. Always wear rubber gloves when working on a battery.

4 Flush the case with water, then wipe dry. Removing the surface grime prevents the build-up of a path where current can leak between the terminals, slowly discharging the battery.

5 Remove each battery cable. Use a terminal puller to avoid having to pry on the battery case, which is easily cracked.

6 Wearing rubber gloves, use a wire brush or battery terminal cleaner to remove corrosion from the terminals and clamps.

7 Once everything is clean, apply a film of petroleum jelly and re-attach the cables. Do not over-tighten the cable clamps, as you can crack the case or break the clamps.

8 Remove the battery hold-downs, remove any corrosion, and reinstall. Do not over-tighten.

A battery charger (A) is a useful auto shop accessory. It will allow you to easily recharge a battery. Always remove the battery cell covers (B) when using a battery charger.

TIP:

Removing a battery cable might knock out your radio station presets, the dashboard clock and other functions. A battery memory keeper, available at auto parts stores, will prevent this.

MASTERCRAFT

BASIC HAND TOOLS

- flex-head ratchet handle
- spark plug cable puller
- spark plug socket
- extension bar
- feeler gauge
- gapping tool

NEEDED MATERIALS

- spray lubricant
- spark plug socket
- masking tape
- silicone paste

If the engine has more than 80,000 km (50,000 mi) on it, replacing the spark plugs, plug cables, rotor and distributor cap will give you better fuel mileage, easier starting, less pollution, smoother operation and more power. Before you decide to tackle this project, first spend some time under the hood. You must have access to all the spark plugs – unfortunately, some manufacturers bury one or more spark plugs under other things, making access difficult.

Check the plug cables. If they are brittle, greasy, cracked or look burned, they are definitely due for a replacement. This applies no matter what the mileage. Never just replace one bad plug wire; replace the whole set. Visit your auto centre and get good quality plug cables that are exact replacements. The cable should be completely assembled and designed specifically for your engine and vehicle. A new distributor cap and rotor are next. Again, be sure to get only specified replacements.

For spark plugs, choose a premium brand, making sure they are specified for your model year and engine size. Platinum plugs will last longer without needing replacement, typically 160,000 km (100,000 mi), while conventional plugs are used up by 48,000 km (30,000 mi).

How to Replace Spark Plugs, Plug Cables, Rotor & Distributor Cap

1 Let the engine cool down before replacing spark plugs. A hot plug will have expanded; you can damage the head by removing the plug while it is hot, especially with engines that have aluminum heads.

2 To prevent confusion, use masking tape and a mark to label each old plug wire and its corresponding end on the distributor. Work on only one spark plug and cable at a time, completing all steps before moving on to the next plug.

3 Gently twist and pull the spark plug boot, not the cable itself, until it comes free. A spark plug cable puller will help.

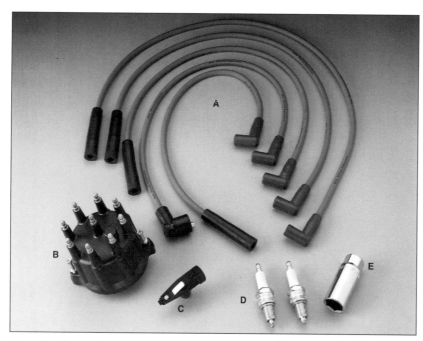

Spark plug cables (A), distributor cap (B), rotor (C), spark plugs (D), spark plug socket (E).

4 Once free, remove the old spark plug using a spark plug socket and a ratchet handle (you may need an extension bar to do so).

5 Set the electrode gap on the new spark plug to the specified measurement in your owner's manual. Do not assume that the new plugs are correctly gapped.

6 Spray a bit of lubricant onto the new plug's threads, and install it. Do not over-tighten.

7 Remove the old plug cable from the distributor, and find its replacement.

8 Match the position of the new distributor cap to the old one, and attach the new plug cable to the corresponding terminal.

9 Remove the old distributor cap, lift off the rotor and replace it with the new one, followed by the new distributor cap.

10 Repeat steps 3-8 for the remaining plugs and cables.

TIP:
Remove any parts needing replacement, and take them to the auto parts store to make sure you get exact replacements. This also allows you to buy whatever additional parts, gaskets, tools or supplies you discover you need.

With use, a rotor's contact edge becomes pitted and corroded (A) making poor contact with the contact points in the distributor cap, which also deteriorate with use. A new rotor will make proper contact with the contact points (B) in a new distributor cap.

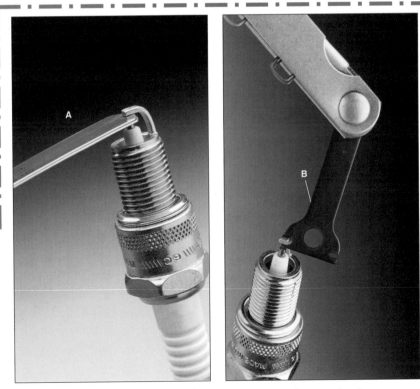

A feeler gauge (A) will help you determine the spark plug gap to the specifications found in your owner's manual. The gapping tool (B) will help you adjust the spark plug gap.

Jump-starting a Vehicle

Every vehicle should have a good pair of jumper cables stowed away. There are a lot of ways to kill a battery: A moment's forgetfulness that leaves the lights on for hours; extremely cold weather; a failing alternator; a battery dying from old age; even some engine problems that require repeated engine cranking. Having a good set of jumper cables may make the difference between getting home or being stranded.

Buy medium to heavy-duty jumper cables. The features you want are:
- Either 4- or 6-gauge wire
- 16' to 20' long
- Tangle-proof design

Have clamps that are colour-coded, clearly labelled, and will work with either top-, front- or side-mounted battery terminals.

To get all of these features, you'll pay more, but it is a good investment, as they should last your whole driving career.

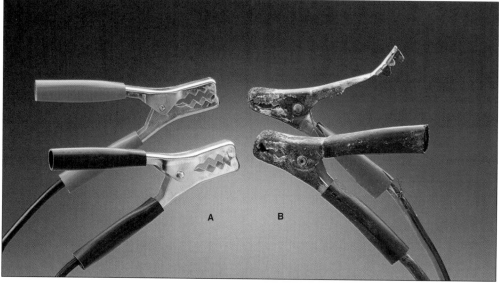

*Jumper cables that **work well** and are safe to use (A) will have clamps in good condition, with rubber covers on the handles and no exposed wire where the cables meet the clamps. Jumper cables in poor condition (B) are not safe to use.*

How to Jump-start a Vehicle

WARNING: Never smoke around batteries – they produce hydrogen, an explosive gas.

1 Check the dead battery. If it is obviously cracked, frozen or its built-in "eye" is clear or bright yellow, don't attempt to jump-start it. The battery is dead and can't be revived. A frozen battery, if jumped, can explode.

2 Park the helper vehicle so it is close, but not touching the car that won't start.

3 Turn off lights, accessories and the ignition switch in both vehicles.

4 Place both transmissions in Park or Neutral and engage the parking brake.

5 Connect a red jumper cable clamp (marked + or POS) to the positive battery terminal (marked +) of the dead battery.

6 Attach the other red clamp to the positive terminal of the helper vehicle's battery. **NOTE:** Once the red clamps are attached to the battery terminals never let the black clamps touch anything else, including each other or you, before they are properly attached for jumping.

7 On the helper vehicle, attach the black cable clamp (marked – or NEG) to the negative battery terminal (marked –).

8 Connect the other black clamp to a metal part on the engine of the dead vehicle – the alternator bracket or an engine mount work well. **NOTE:** Do not attach it to the dead battery terminal, as sparks may result, possibly causing the battery to explode.

9 To keep gases inside, put a damp rag over the vent holes on both batteries.

10 Start the helper vehicle and speed the engine up a bit, then try starting the dead vehicle.

11 If nothing happens, and you are sure the clamps are making contact, wait a few minutes and try again. Be careful not to flood the engine.

12 Once the other vehicle is running, disconnect the jumper cables in this order:

❏ 1st black clamp (negative) from dead vehicle.
❏ 2nd black clamp from helper vehicle. **NOTE:** Remember, do not let the black clamps touch each other or anything else.
❏ 3rd red clamp (positive) from the helper vehicle.
❏ 4th red clamp from dead vehicle.

Vehicle with dead battery requiring jumping.

Helper vehicle to provide the jumping power.

MASTERCRAFT

BASIC HAND TOOLS

- Torx or other specialty screwdriver

NEEDED MATERIALS

- lightweight lubricant
- electrical contact cleaner

TIP:

Many service stations and repair shops have places where you can drive up to check whether your headlights are aimed properly. Halogen headlights are stationary and do not require aiming.

Replacing Sealed-beam & Halogen Headlights

When a headlight burns out, first determine which type of headlight system you have. In a sealed-beam system (A), you replace the entire headlight. In a halogen system (B), you only replace the bulb.

How to Replace Sealed-beam Headlights

1 Loosen the screws and remove the trim panel surrounding the headlight (photo opposite page left).

2 Identify the headlight adjusting screws, usually the ones with springs around them.

3 Leave those screws alone and remove the others that hold the headlight in place. (These screws may be a specialized type, such as the star-shaped Torx. Your auto parts centre or hardware store sells screwdrivers that fit.) If you cannot find a way to remove the headlight, check your owner's manual for instructions.

4 Pull the headlight forward slightly to expose the electrical connector at its back. If the headlight was flickering, the problem may be a loose connection or corrosion on the contacts, both of which can be fixed without replacement (see page 20).

5 Buy a good quality replacement. If you have standard sealed-beam headlamps, spend the extra few dollars for a set of halogen-type replacements. Halogen sealed-beams produce a much brighter, whiter light.

6 Check for corrosion or dirt before reattaching the connector. Spray electrical contact cleaner into the electrical connector to flush out any corrosion.

7 Spray a lightweight lubricant on the various mounting and adjustment screws to help prevent corrosion.

8 Reattach the electrical connector to the headlight, being careful not to twist and push too hard because it is easy to break off the terminals.

9 Before reinstalling the trim, make sure the new headlight works. While the trim is off, it is also a good time to make sure the headlights are pointing properly (see tip left).

*A **sealed-beam headlight** is usually removed from the front of the vehicle. The trim panel surrounding the headlight and the retaining screws holding the unit in place must be removed first.*

*A **halogen bulb** is removed from the back side of the headlight housing, usually from within the engine compartment. This often can be accomplished without the use of tools.*

How to Replace Halogen Bulbs

1 Instead of looking in front for the trim and retaining screws as you would for sealed-beam headlights, open the hood and check the back of the light. You probably will not need any tools to replace the halogen bulb.

2 With your fingers, twist to unlock the retaining ring, usually a quarter turn to the left. Slide it backwards, exposing the bulb housing assembly.

3 Then simply wiggle the socket straight back to remove it from the headlight housing (photo above right).

4 Lift the plastic locking lug and unplug the burned-out bulb.

5 Hold the new bulb and align the socket in its opening, then push it into place.

6 Slip the retaining ring forward and relock it with a quarter turn to the right.

TIP:
Never touch the glass of a halogen bulb with your bare hands. The oils on your skin will cause the bulb to burn out as soon as it heats up. Instead, hold it with a cloth or tissue while inserting into the socket.

- replacement hoses
- replacement pump
- replacement reservoir
- straight pin or needle

Windshield & Wiper Maintenance

Keeping your windshield clear so you have good visibility while driving is an obvious need. Neglecting this simple issue can cause serious problems when you are on the road.

Keeping Your Windshield Clean

❏ Check the windshield wiper fluid level weekly or every time you fill up with gas. Check it daily when poor weather conditions force you to use fluid frequently.

❏ Replace the rubber blades twice a year or anytime you notice deterioration in performance. Depending on your car you can buy either a blade insert or the entire wiper assembly (photo below). If you have to buy the entire assembly, buy one that will allow you to replace only the blade insert the next time.

❏ Clean the wiper blades when you clean the windshield. Wipe them down with a rag or sponge dipped in washer fluid. Dirty blades will not work well even if the windshield is clean. They also can scratch the glass.

❏ The wiper arm unit must exert enough pressure to keep the wipers clearing the windshield properly. Pull the arm unit away from the windshield about 1", then

TIP:
Keep wax off of the windshield (which many drive-through car washes apply as part of their process). Wax will prevent wipers from properly cleaning the windshield. If wax is applied to the windshield, scrub it off with a wax-removing detergent.

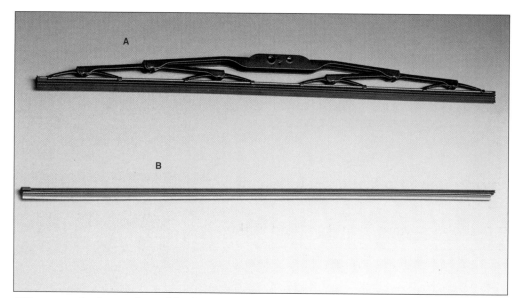

When replacing wiper blades, *replace the entire wiper assembly (A) if the old one is rusting or broken. Otherwise you only need to replace the blade (B) which usually fits into a clip on the wiper assembly.*

release it. It should snap back onto the windshield. Adjust the tension if it does not do so (check your owner's manual for the method to do this). If you are unable to create enough tension, replace the arm unit; changing blades will not help the problem.

❏ Remember to clean the inside of the windshield. A greasy film accumulates on the interior surface of the glass (which can make the glass fog up very easily). A foam glass cleaner is much easier to use on the inside than regular liquid cleaners.

engine running. Operate the washer and listen to the pump (this will be easier if you have a helper).

5 If the pump is silent, check its electrical connections to make sure they are free of corrosion and in proper contact. If these check out, replace the pump (photo left), either with the manufacturer's replacement or a generic model (which may require some adjustments to make it fit).

6 If the pump is fine, disconnect the hoses from the nozzles and turn the washer on. If fluid does not come out of the hoses, then they are blocked, either between the reservoir and pump or between the pump and nozzles. Replace all of the hoses.

7 If the fluid sprays out of the hoses, then the nozzles are clogged. Clear the nozzle openings with a needle or fine wire (photo below). You also can try clearing it with a blast of spray lubricant.

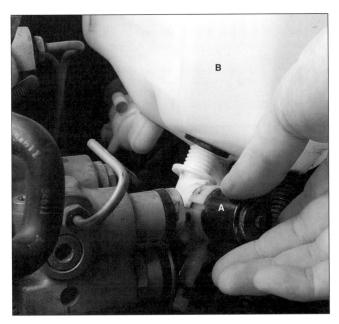

Replacing the wiper pump (A) is relatively simple. It usually is found at the base of the wiper fluid reservoir (B).

How to Repair a Windshield Washer System

1 Make sure there is washer fluid in the reservoir.

2 Check the screen on the tube carrying fluid from the tank to the pump and make sure it is not clogged with sediment.

3 If the reservoir is leaking, replace it with a new one.

4 To check for proper pump operation, turn the ignition key on but without the

Use a straight pin or needle to clear a clogged nozzle opening.

- pry bar
- wrench set or ratchet/socket set
- Robo-Grip pliers/adjustable wrench

Adjusting or Replacing Drive Belts

A loud squealing from under the hood usually indicates a loose drive or accessory belt. Using a work light, check both sides of the belt for cracked or frayed edges, heavy oil deposits, splits or glazing (glossy areas).

How to Adjust or Replace Drive Belts

1 Inspect the belt. If any of the conditions described at left exist, replace the belt immediately. Make sure to buy a replacement that is the same length and width (the size of the "v").

2 Check proper belt tension when the engine is cold. Push down in the centre of the longest span of the belt. It should move about ½". Adjust the belt if it moves more or less than this.

3 Identify the nuts and bolts that secure the belt-driven device (such as an alternator). Loosen these bolts so the device moves freely, then retighten the bolts slightly.

4 To loosen belt tension, push slightly on the belt-driven device. If replacing the belt, push on the device until the belt is loose enough to remove from the pulleys. Double-check the replacement to make sure it is the correct size, then install the new belt over the pulleys.

5 To tighten belt tension, carefully wedge a pry bar between the device and a solid part of the engine, but not where it could damage other components.

6 Pull on the pry bar to tighten the belt until the correct tension is reached, then retighten the adjustment and pivot bolts. Never over-tighten a belt. Too much tension will cause early failure of water pump and alternator bearings.

7 Start the car and check for proper belt operation.

8 If you installed a new belt, recheck the tension after the engine has run for a few hours.

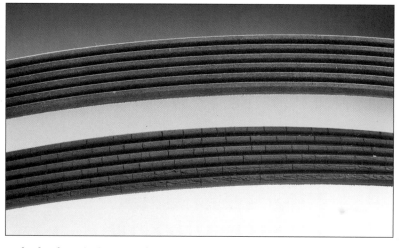

A belt that is in good condition (top) will not have cracks, frayed edges or pieces missing, which indicate a belt requiring replacement (bottom).

Check for proper belt tension by pressing on the middle of the longest section between pulleys that you can reach.

Identifying & Fixing Leaks

Few things cause more concern than a pool of liquid under your car. Leaks are relatively easy to identify, and once you have done that, you will likely know how to deal with them. Often just tightening a clamp or a bolt is all you need to do. In some cases, the leak is actually a normal condition.

Guide to Identifying Leaks:

To make sure you properly identify the leak, place a plastic container where it is occurring. Dribble a few drops onto a piece of white paper so you can see what colour it is. Use the following guide to identify the leak:

❏ **Antifreeze/coolant:** Comes in three colours, green, yellow or orange, unless it is very old, in which case it will be rusty brown. It has a sweet odour. ADVICE: Find and fix the leak.

❏ **Automatic transmission fluid:** Typically light red or brownish red, very lightweight oil. Compare it to what you get from the transmission dip-stick to be sure. ADVICE: Find and fix the leak immediately.

❏ **Battery acid:** This fluid is hard to miss because of its rotten-egg odour. It is also highly corrosive, so keep it off your skin and clothing. ADVICE: Replace the battery, as there is no fix for this.

❏ **Brake fluid:** Clear, thin and slick, you might even mistake it for water. ADVICE: Leaking brake fluid is a danger sign. Have your vehicle towed to a service centre.

❏ **Diesel fuel:** If you have a diesel engine, you know what it looks and smells like. It is nearly the same as home heating oil. ADVICE: Find and fix the leak immediately.

❏ **Gasoline:** Hard to mistake the sharp, unmistakable odour for anything else. Any gasoline leakage is a potential fire hazard. ADVICE: Find and fix the leak immediately.

❏ **Gear oil:** This dark, heavy oil is used in manual transmissions, axles, differentials and other spots. ADVICE: Find the source and have it fixed.

❏ **Grease:** If it is thick and black, it is grease. ADVICE: Some minor leakage after lube jobs is normal. Otherwise, have a professional check for the problem.

❏ **Motor oil:** A medium- to dark-coloured oil that lubricates the engine. ADVICE: Small spots indicate leaks that tightening bolts or replacing gaskets will fix. Look for oil stains on the engine to help locate the source. A pool of oil is serious; have your vehicle towed to a service centre.

❏ **Power-steering fluid:** Older vehicles use auto-transmission fluid, but newer models use a fluid that looks like fresh motor oil, only thinner and with a different colour. ADVICE: If it has turned silver-grey, there is likely a failure within the power-steering system. In any case, a professional repair is required.

❏ **Shock-absorber fluid:** More likely to show up as a dark oil stain on the shock itself. ADVICE: There is no fix, so replace the shock, and most likely all of them, to ensure proper vehicle handling.

❏ **Water:** If you find what seems like a pool of water under your vehicle on a hot day, and you have been running the air-conditioner, this is simply condensation draining away. ADVICE: This is completely normal; no need to fix.

❏ **Windshield washer solution:** Typically blue and often smells of alcohol. ADVICE: Usually this is a sign of a leaking hose or fluid reservoir. Find the source of the leak and fix as soon as possible, particularly during inclement weather.

Vital Fluids

Gasoline, motor oil and antifreeze/coolant are your vehicle's lifeblood. If neglected they can cause major repair headaches. Here are a few things to remember:

❏ Using a higher octane fuel than specified in your owner's manual is a waste of money. The only major difference between grades of gasoline is the higher anti-knock quality (octane) of premium. Buying gasoline that has a higher octane rating than your car needs provides absolutely zero benefits. Higher octane does not produce more power, contrary to advertising claims. Most of today's vehicles are designed to use 87-octane unleaded regular. If in doubt, check your owner's manual.

❏ Premium fuel is not a better grade of fuel and does not contain more additives or detergents than regular gasoline.

❏ Motor oil cleans, lubricates, cools and cushions moving engine parts, while holding sludge and chemical contaminates in suspension until it is changed. It also has an effect on fuel economy. An engine produces tremendous heat. Without motor oil, an engine would be severely damaged within minutes. Heat breaks down motor oil's lubricating qualities and should be changed along with the oil filter every 5,000 to 8,000 km (3,000 to 5,000 mi).

❏ Because of constant advancements, it is not necessary to switch oil weights during the winter if you are using 5W-30 or 10W-30. In fact the "W" indicates the oil meets cold weather viscosity demands.

❏ Motor oil will turn dark after 5,000 km (3,000 mi), but dirty oil is simply proof that it is doing its job of keeping the by-products of combustion in suspension so they can be drained from the engine.

❏ Synthetic oil, which has been around for over 40 years, is formulated from hydro-carbons manufactured from crude petro-leum or natural gas. Synthetics do not thicken under extreme cold and can better withstand severe heat. While synthet-ics are advertised as maintaining their lubricating qualities for 40,000 km (25,000 mi), much longer than conventional oil, you still must replace the filters at shorter intervals to remove trapped contaminates.

❏ A mix of 50% glycol antifreeze and 50% water is called coolant and protects your cooling systems from freezing to –37°C (–34°F) and overheating. Most car manufacturers recommend flushing and refilling the cooling system with new coolant every two years or 40,000 km (25,000 mi). Although the temperature protection will still be –37°C (–34°F), the coolant's anti-corrosive and lubricating additives wear out. Excessive corrosion can cause radiator damage, a clogged heater core, ruin the thermostat or cause the water pump to fail.

A B C

New oil (A) is light in colour and clear, used oil that is still functional (B) is darker in colour than new oil but still clear, oil that needs replacing (C) is very dark to black in colour and is no longer clear.

Oil & Filter Change

The oil and filter change is the most basic of automotive maintenance tasks, yet one of the most important. Be sure to have everything you will need on hand.

How to Change Your Oil & Filter

1 If the engine is cold, run it for a few minutes to warm and thin the oil. Then shut it down and remove the oil filler cap on the top of the engine.

2 Position the drain pan under the plug and remove the drain plug using a ratchet and socket (photo below left). Let the old oil drain out while you clean the drain plug.

3 When the old oil has slowed to a trickle, use a rag to clean off the area around the drain plug, then reinstall it. It should be tight, but do not over-tighten or you will damage the threads and oil pan. **NOTE:** Replace the drain plug every year to prevent leaks.

4 Position the drain pan under the filter and loosen the filter enough for oil to come out in a stream (photo below right).

5 After the oil has drained away from the filter, remove it all the way and clean the area where the filter attaches with a clean rag. **NOTE:** Look for any sign of a rubber gasket stuck in place.

6 Use some clean oil to lubricate the rubber gasket on the new filter, then spin it into place. Do not over-tighten. A quarter turn past where it first starts to feel tight is all you need.

7 Pour in the fresh oil (check your owner's manual for the proper amount). When opening bottles of oil, completely remove any paper seals or plastic rings to prevent them from falling into the engine.

8 Start up the engine for just a minute. On startup, get out and check under the engine to make sure there is not a surprise leak.

9 If there are no leaks, let the engine run for a minute or two, then shut it off. Wait another few minutes, then check the oil level with the dipstick.

RECOMMENDED HAND TOOLS

- oil filter
- wrench set or ratchet/socket set
- safety goggles

NEEDED MATERIALS

- drain pan with funnel
- rags
- oil
- filter
- rubber gloves

TIP:
If your oil filter is easily visible, use a permanent marker to write the date and mileage of the oil/filter change. If it is not, keep a log of oil/filter changes in the glove compartment. Either will serve as a quick reminder of when the next change is due.

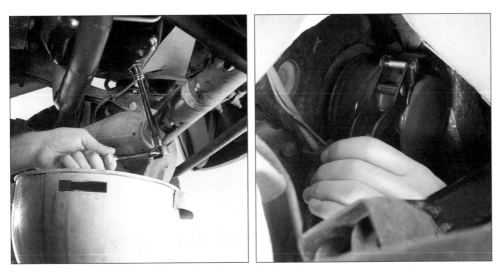

Steering & Suspension

If roads were smooth, straight and flat, keeping control of our cars would be simple. We wouldn't need shock absorbers, struts, springs or extensive wheel alignment procedures, to name just a few of the items involved. But that's not the way our roads are, so you need to understand what the steering and suspension systems do:

❑ Provide a smooth, quiet, comfortable ride by allowing the tires and wheels to move up and down with minimal body movement.

❑ Reduce excessive body roll during cornering.

❑ Hold the tires tight to the road surface, even after colliding with bumps and potholes.

❑ Prevent excessive body squat – the vehicle pitching up or down during heavy acceleration or braking.

❑ Allow the front wheels to be turned from side to side, and work with the steering system to maintain wheel alignment.

Depending on your vehicle's make and model, it can have four shocks (most rear wheel drive vehicles), front struts and rear shocks (front and rear wheel drive vehicles with semi-independent suspension), or four struts (front wheel drive vehicles with independent suspension).

Checking Steering & Suspension

When shocks and struts wear out, you will experience bouncing and noise going over bumps (although weak springs can also cause the same symptoms). A simple, but not terribly accurate test is to push down on the end of the vehicle as hard and as far down as you can. When you let up, the car should come to rest after only one bounce.

The only accurate way to test a shock absorber/strut assembly is to remove it from the car,

A shock absorber (A) assists the coil spring (B) in diminishing road bumps. A strut system (C) incorporates both spring and shock suppression in one unit.

mount it in a vise and operate the shock/strut by hand to determine if there's adequate resistance. This testing is almost never done because of the work and time involved. Generally, if the shocks or struts have more than 64,000 km (40,000 mi) on them, you're best off just replacing them.

Choosing the Type of Shock Absorber You Need:

❑ Most standard shocks use hydraulic oil to smooth out the vehicle's ride.

❑ Better gas-charged shocks use low pressure hydrogen gas to help keep the oil from foaming during continuous up-and-down movement.

❑ Load-levelling shocks have a special air valve to allow adjustment when extra weight is added.

❑ Adjustable shocks allow you to reach under the car to turn the shock absorber's outer tower to set the feel from hard to soft.

The most common replacement shock is the load levelling or air shock. Compressed air is added to the shocks helping raise the level of the car when carrying additional passengers or towing a trailer.

Whenever you're under the vehicle performing any type of maintenance, always visually inspect the front and rear suspension system. Look for binding, dry, torn or rotted rubber parts, signs of looseness or wear, damaged or missing parts and lack of lubrication.

Most problems that you feel through the steering wheel are caused by suspension or alignment problems. But if your vehicle steering is harder than normal, have it checked for damaged steering components. If you have power steering, first check the power steering fluid reservoir attached to the power steering unit to make sure it contains the proper amount of fluid (photo below). Add more if it is low and check it again in a few weeks. If it is low again, check for leaks in the hoses that lead to the front wheels.

Don't forget to check for the proper level of fluid *in the power steering reservoir when doing routine maintenance on your vehicle. If you are experiencing steering control that feels harder than usual, check here first.*

Brake Maintenance

Ideally you should have your brakes checked at least once a year, even if none of the symptoms on these pages are present. Inspecting your brakes during routine maintenance only takes a few extra minutes and will alert you to potential problems before they become dangerous. When replacing your brake shoes or pads, always use high quality replacements.

Symptoms Indicating Your Brakes May Need Servicing:

❏ Rhythmical vibrations or pulsation in the brake pedal (unless your vehicle has an anti-lock brake system, where these pulses are normal) could mean the brake rotors or drums are warped (out-of-round).

❏ If the brake warning light on the instrument panel stays lit after the engine is started, the brake system could have a serious hydraulic pressure problem.

❏ A light squeak when the brakes are not being used is the brake wear indicators announcing it is time for a routine brake service.

❏ Brakes that pull the car to one side, grab suddenly, drag or lock up prematurely are all dangerous. Have a mechanic check for hydraulic fluid leaking onto the brakes, sticking disc brake calipers, collapsed brake hoses or wheel cylinder problems.

❏ An occasional squeak or squeal from disc brakes under light braking is normal, but any loud screeching, grinding or shuddering may mean either worn-out brake pads or brake shoes that are scoring the rotors or drums.

❏ A squeaking or clicking noise from the rear end when releasing the brake pedal signals a lack of lithium grease on the rear brake shoe backing plate. If allowed to continue, grooves will be worn into the plates and the brakes will not return to their normal position, causing overheating and unexpected wheel lock-up.

Drum brake shoes that are in good condition (A) still have adequate friction material. The material has been worn away to expose brake wear indicators on shoes that require replacement (B).

The surface of a disc brake rotor should be smooth and clean (B) to provide proper resistance for the friction material on the brake pads. A rotor that becomes scored, pitted or covered with rust (A) must be resurfaced or replaced (if there is not enough metal left on the rotor for it to be resurfaced).

❏ Changes in the feel of your brake pedal may also indicate trouble. A pedal that is now too high or difficult to press down could be signalling a power brake problem.

❏ A constant hissing when the brake pedal is held down means a vacuum leak in the power brake booster.

❏ A soft pedal that goes nearly to the floor may be caused by poorly adjusted brakes or a serious brake system failure.

❏ A spongy-feeling brake pedal often means air is trapped in the brake system. Often, just draining out some of the brake fluid to remove the air and then adjusting the brakes solves this problem.

❏ Dog-tracking is when both rear wheels seem to lock up at the same time when braking while the car is cold. This usually occurs after having front pads replaced.

Pads and shoes from different manufacturers are often made from dissimilar materials (metallic, semi-metallic or organic) and so they heat up at different rates. Dog-tracking is usually a temporary condition that corrects itself after a few miles of driving allow the new pads to heat up.

❏ Even though a car pulling to one side during breaking is usually caused by a brake problem of some kind, have your repair shop inspect the suspension carefully. A loose, worn or weak suspension part, or a front or rear end out of alignment can cause a car to pull to one side when braking.

Disc brake pads that are in good condition (A) still have adequate friction material. On pads that require replacement (B), the friction material has been worn away to expose brake wear indicators.

Taking Care of Tires

Tires have a great deal to do with keeping your vehicle safely on the road, but a relatively small amount of tire actually is touching the road while you drive. It is very important that tires are well maintained to keep you moving dependably and safely. Tires are not cheap either; good maintenance and driving habits will provide the best value.

While there is a wide variety of choices in sizes and styles of tires, bias-ply, belted-bias and radial are the three types of tire construction used today. Radial tires are the most common type because they offer lower rolling resistance, providing better mileage and improved cornering and braking. They also can wear longer: Top of the line radials may last 100,000 km (60,000 mi) or more, compared to 40,000 km (25,000 mi) for bias-ply and 56,000 km (35,000 mi) for belted-bias. Check with your tire dealer to determine which type and style of tire are best suited to your needs when you need replacements.

Keep in mind that your driving style and road conditions significantly affect tire wear. Other factors affecting tires are the condition of the vehicle's braking and suspension systems, tire inflation and wheel alignment. Except for road conditions, you can control these factors to obtain the longest and most dependable use from your tires.

Tread that is separating from the rest of the tire indicates a tire that needs replacing immediately. Also check the alignment.

General Tire Maintenance

❑ Check general tire condition when you fill up with gas. Look for cuts, bubbles, separating tread (photo left), bulges or cracking on the sidewalls, nails and abnormal wear.

❑ Check tire pressure monthly. Proper inflation not only protects the tires, it also gives you the best gas mileage.

❑ Check tread depth at least twice a year, depending on the number of miles you drive. Tire wear indicators are bars that show up as smooth strips of rubber across the face of the tire when the tread is less than 1/8"-deep. They indicate that it is time to get a new set of tires.

❑ Remember the spare! It is easy to overlook, but at least twice a year check its condition and pressure. Also do this before you go on a long trip. Follow the manufacturer's instructions if your car is equipped with a mini spare.

- Have the front and rear alignment checked at least once a year. Driving on rough roads may necessitate more frequent checks.

- New tires should always be installed in pairs. If you are purchasing only one pair, they should be installed on the front axle.

- Never mix radial tires with bias-ply or belted-bias tires. Doing so will throw your vehicle out of alignment.

- Have your tires rotated every 8,000 to 10,000 km (5,000 to 6,000 mi). Rotation evens out tire wear and will help provide the longest, safest use.

- Installing tires larger or smaller than the vehicle manufacturer's recommendations could affect speedometer calibration.

- If a radial tire picks up a nail, it should not be plugged from the outside. Instead, remove the tire from the wheel and have a hot or cold vulcanizing patch applied from the inside. While more costly and time consuming, since the wheel will require rebalancing once the tire is remounted, this is the safest and most durable repair. This should be done by a professional.

Identifying Tire Wear Problems

- If both edges are worn (photo right, top), this indicates underinflation. Properly inflate the tire.

- If centre tread is worn (photo right, middle), this indicates overinflation. Properly inflate the tire.

- Tires worn on one edge (photo right, bottom) indicate poor alignment. Have the wheels aligned.

Worn tread at edges *indicates underinflation.*

Worn centre tread *indicates overinflation.*

Worn tread on one edge *indicates poor alignment.*

❑ Tires worn unevenly (photo below), with bald spots, cups or scallops indicate poor alignment. Have the wheels aligned.

❑ Saw-toothed or ragged wear pattern indicates rough, excessive braking. Drive with slower speeds and pump brakes.

❑ Only edges of front tires worn indicates curves taken too fast. Drive with slower speed through curves.

❑ Squealing on curves indicates poor alignment, underinflation or excessive speed. Check wear on tread as indicated above and make proper adjustments.

Tools for changing tires: *hydraulic trolley jack (A), axle/jack stands (B), typical jack provided by vehicle manufacturer (C), 4-arm spanner (D), torque wrench (E).*

Uneven wear, *such as cupping or scalloping, indicates poor alignment.*

Tires & Winter Driving

❑ If you only use two snow tires on a rear wheel drive vehicle, they should be the same size and design as the other tires on the vehicle and should be installed on the rear axle. (All-weather radials, rather than snow tires, are recommended for all tires on front wheel drive vehicles.) If you choose to use a complete set of snow tires, make sure they meet manufacturer's recommendations for your vehicle (and remember to have a proper spare).

❑ Check snow tire condition and pressure before mounting them at the beginning of the winter season.

❑ Check tread wear and condition of other tires when mounting only two snow tires.

❑ Consider buying another set of wheels and permanently mounting the tires on them. This will make changing to snow tires each season easier.

❑ Unless it is an emergency situation, never drive with a snow tire and any other type of tire on the same axle. This can cause serious alignment problems and damage to the differential or transaxle.

TIP:
Tire dressing and protectant products don't just keep tires looking great. The silicone- or rubber-based compounds they contain will protect the sidewalls from cracking.

Changing a Tire

Whether it is because of a flat tire on the highway, the need to rotate the tires to prolong their life or installing snow tires before winter, knowing how to change a tire is an essential skill. Prepare your car in advance for a possible flat tire away from home. Do not rely on the factory-supplied lug wrench, which is often too short to allow you to loosen tight lug nuts. Buy a large 4-arm spanner or torque wrench and carry along an aerosol can of rust-penetrating lubricant. You may also want to replace the supplied jack with a better unit. If you are changing tires in your garage, use jack stands and be sure to coat each wheel stud with anti-seize lubricant before installing lug nuts as it prevents corrosion from locking the nuts to the wheel. Never use a pneumatic wrench to tighten lug nuts because you could possibly warp the wheel if you over-tighten.

How to Change a Flat Tire

1 Park on a level, solid section safely out of traffic.

2 Put on the parking brake and place transmission in Park (automatics) or Reverse (manuals). Have passengers get out and stand safely away from the vehicle and traffic.

3 If you can find something (a large rock) to chock the wheel at the end opposite the flat, do so.

4 Get out everything you need. Ensure your spare is in good shape before you go to the trouble of removing the flat.

5 Remove any hub cap or wheel covers. Spray the lug nuts with penetrating oil or other lubricant. Give it a few minutes to work, then using the spanner, loosen each lug nut.

6 Position the jack. The correct jacking points are shown in the owner's manual. If in doubt, place the jack under any portion of the frame near the flat tire. Jack the vehicle up until the tire is about to leave the ground.

7 Remove the lug nuts.

8 Continue jacking until you can pull the wheel off and replace with the spare. Adjust jack as needed.

9 Spin on the lug nuts by hand, then use the spanner until the spare is bolted in place.

10 Lower the jack until the spare just touches the ground then tighten each lug nut in a star pattern or, if there are only four lug nuts, tighten them in opposing pairs.

11 Remove whatever wheel chocks you used, load everything into the vehicle and go to the nearest service station to repair the tire and check the pressure of the spare. If you have a space-saver spare, watch your speed as they are not intended for extended or high-speed use.

RECOMMENDED HAND TOOLS

- 4-arm spanner or torque wrench
- jack
- axle/jack stands
- wheel chocks

NEEDED MATERIALS

- rust-penetrating lubricant
- anti-seize lubricant

TIP:

When changing a flat tire, safety is the most critical consideration. This means getting your vehicle as far onto the shoulder as possible. Light flares (which should be in your emergency kit) and put on your warning blinkers. If the road is narrow or very busy, it may be wise to drive slowly on the shoulder until you find a safer spot or an exit. It is better to damage a wheel than risk personal injury.

Muffler Repairs

Hopefully, the first symptom you have of a deteriorating muffler is the sudden increase in exhaust noise. This indicates it is time to replace the muffler. This is also a good time to visually inspect the rest of the exhaust system. Leaks release dangerous fumes which may enter the passenger compartment of your vehicle.

If you hear a loud scraping sound, this means some portion of the exhaust system is dragging. Stop immediately; the dragging pipe or muffler can wedge itself under your vehicle and cause serious damage, or break loose and get in the path of another vehicle.

Drive your vehicle safely off the road and up onto a curb, if possible, to raise the side where the muffler is. Never attempt to work under a vehicle that is supported only by the supplied tire jack. Shut off the engine, and wait for 20 to 30 minutes if you can. Exhaust parts will be very hot. Wear gloves or use a thick layer of rags to protect your hands, even after waiting.

Usually a broken hanger is the culprit. You need to use some rope, heavy string, elastic cords or a straightened coat hanger to tie up and support the exhaust system long enough to get it properly repaired. Wrap the cord or wire around the tailpipe near the rear bumper. Then feed the wire through any nearby bracket or frame piece. Do not wrap anything around the driveshaft, hoses or other parts that will not support the weight.

This is a quick fix intended to get you home or to a service centre where the proper repair can be made.

Replacing a Muffler

❑ When working on the muffler, raise the car and support it on axle/jack stands and/or ramps. The axle/jack stands should be positioned at places on the frame.

❑ Before working on the exhaust system, make sure all the parts are cold. This will be safer for you and cold parts are easier to work on – if the engine has been running, allow it to cool down for at least three hours.

❑ Common joints, such as that between the muffler and tailpipe, need a coat of exhaust system joint sealer before they are clamped together. The sealer, not the clamp, prevents leaks.

❑ Separating the tailpipe from the muffler is often difficult. Engine heat often fuses the metal end connections together. You may need to replace both the muffler and the tailpipe.

❑ This job may involve loosening frozen fasteners. Saturate nuts and bolts with penetrating oil and allow it to work for 10 minutes. If you still cannot release the fastener, cut it away with a cold chisel or hacksaw.

Exhaust system: catalytic converter (A), clamp (B), muffler (C), tailpipe (D), hanger (E).

Preparing for Summer Driving

Summer can be as tough on your car as winter is. There are several things you can do to ensure problem-free driving during the hot summer months.

Summer Preparations

❏ Have your air conditioning system checked for the proper refrigerant charge. The first scorching hot day is not the time to find your A/C system blowing hot instead of cold. Be certain your service centre adds the correct type of refrigerant to your system if it is in need of a recharge. Do not attempt to recharge your A/C; instead call a professional.

❏ Check the operation of the electric cooling fan and the thermostatic fan clutch. For non-electric powered fans do this by spinning the fan blade, with the engine off and cold. When cold, the fan should spin freely.

❏ Check the seal on the radiator cap. Caps cost only a few dollars, but are an essential component in the cooling system. If in doubt, replace with a new one that has the same temperature rating.

❏ Carry a gallon of water in the trunk. If your engine starts to overheat, open the windows, shut off the air conditioning and turn on the heater. Running the heater will disperse excess heat from the engine. If you are stopped in traffic for long periods, pop open the hood to release heat built up from the engine compartment. Just be sure to securely shut the hood before you resume driving.

CAUTION: Remember, never remove the radiator cap from an overheating engine. You could be seriously burned. Let the engine cool down first.

Flush bugs and dirt out of the radiator and the air conditioning condenser with a garden hose. Work from the engine side, directing the stream of water out through the radiator.

❏ Check all hoses when the engine is cold for flexibility and wear. If they are stiff, leaking or have cracks, then have them replaced before they leave you stranded. In most cases, you can replace the hoses yourself.

❏ If you tow a trailer, consider adding an external automatic transmission oil cooler to your car or truck if it is not so equipped. They are relatively inexpensive. The extra strain of pulling a trailer can easily cause the transmission oil to overheat, and burn out the transmission, which is very expensive to fix.

❏ Try to keep your vehicle out of the blazing sun whenever possible. The excess heat will damage the paint, fade interior fabrics, cause the windshield wiper blades to stick to the glass and cause tires to dry out and crack. If you have a vinyl top, it is a good idea to treat it with a preservative regularly during the summer.

Preparing for Winter Driving

Cold, snowy winters are tough on all vehicles. Wintertime travel can be risky if severe cold or heavy snow leaves you stranded. You can reduce the chances of having problems by preparing your car.

Winter Preparations

❏ Change oil and filter if necessary. Make sure to use the weight of oil your owner's manual specifies for your vehicle; starting will be easiest if the proper oil is in the engine.

❏ Check coolant for a 50/50 antifreeze and water mix, which protects down to -40°C (-40°F). If the coolant is more than 2 years or 40,000 km (24,000 mi) old, drain, flush and refill.

❏ Check hoses and drive belts for cracks, fraying or obvious signs of age. Replace any that are more than 4 years old. Check belt tension.

❏ Clean and check battery cable connections and battery water level. If the battery is old, replace it now, rather than having it strand you on a bitterly cold night.

❏ Check all fluid levels (oil, transmission, brakes, antifreeze, windshield washer). Make sure windshield cleaner is the type that withstands cold temperatures. Also be certain that transmission fluid is fresh since the strain of trying to get 'unstuck' can burn up a transmission.

❏ Replace wiper blades with fresh ones, perhaps with winter blades that are more resistant to freezing up.

❏ Check all tires, including the spare, for adequate thread depth, cuts, cracks or other damage. Put on snow tires or all-season radials if appropriate. Inflate to recommended pressure. Replace any tires that are worn. **NOTE:** If only buying two new tires, be sure they go on the front of the car for better handling.

❏ Check all lights and turn signals, replacing any that are burnt out or weak.

❏ Lubricate all door locks with spray lubricant to prevent freeze-ups.

❏ To reduce fogging, clean the inside of the windshield. For perfectly clean glass, use Brasso metal polish – supermarkets carry this – followed by windshield washer fluid.

❏ Lightly lubricate door/trunk rubber gaskets with a silicone paste, but keep it away from the paint.

❏ Test the heater and defroster.

❏ If you have been experiencing any other problems, have them fixed before the cold weather really hits.

Use an antifreeze hydrometer to check to be sure you have the proper level of protection.

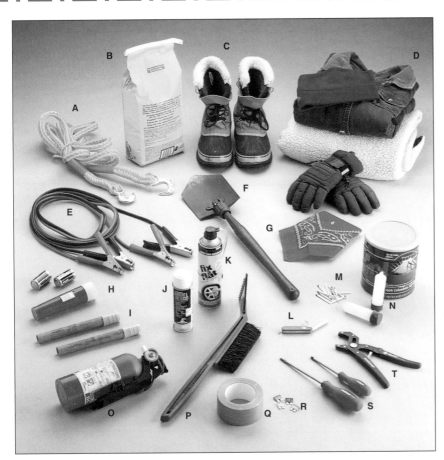

Emergency kit: tow strap (A), traction aid (B), boots (C), extra clothing, gloves, blankets, plastic garbage bags (D), jumper cables (E), small shovel (F), bandanna (G), flashlight with spare batteries (H), flares (I), moisture displacement lubricant (J), tire sealer/inflator (K), can opener (L), matches (M), coffee can with candles (N), fire extinguisher (O), windshield scraper/brush (P), duct tape (Q), spare fuses (R), screwdrivers (S), Robo-Grip pliers (T).

Wintertime Trunk Emergency Kit

This list may seem like overkill, however if you get stuck on the side of the road in a blizzard, especially with your family, you will be thankful you assembled this kit. Check its contents at the beginning of each winter.

❑ Quality jumper cables (see page 26) in good condition.
❑ Flashlight and spare batteries.
❑ Emergency flares.
❑ Spare gloves, overalls or jacket, boots, blanket, hat.
❑ Traction aids such as sand, gravel, cat litter, tire chains, tow rope.
❑ Can of tire sealer/inflator. **NOTE:** Get a brand that does not use a flammable propellant.
❑ Moisture displacement lubricant.
❑ Money for a pay phone or invest in a cellular phone.
❑ Windshield scraper and brush.

❑ Small shovel.
❑ Pliers, screwdrivers, jackknife, duct tape, spare fuses.
❑ Candle stubs or canned heat and matches. These provide light, a little warmth and heat to warm liquids.
❑ Large plastic garbage bags – great weather protection.
❑ An orange or bright red bandanna to put on your antenna as a signal.
❑ Some water, dried or canned foods and beverages and a small can opener.
❑ Most of the small parts of this survival kit fit nicely inside a large coffee can. The can itself can be used for heating soups or beverages.
❑ You may also want to pack in your trunk such things as a fire extinguisher, sleeping bag or extra winter clothing, especially if the forecast warns of severe weather such as sub-zero temperatures, blizzards, etc.

AUTO BODY CARE & REPAIR

The big jobs, repairing major collision or rust damage, are best left to professionals. They have the equipment, skills, access to parts and know-how to return your vehicle to like-new condition. They will get it done much quicker than you can, with better results, though it will cost more. This is especially true whenever there is frame damage, a common situation in most collisions. If it requires welding, specialized skills, hydraulic straightening jacks or other equipment, leave it to professionals. In addition, any work covered by insurance should be entrusted to the auto body shop, but the smaller jobs should be well within your capabilities.

Repairing Chips & Scratches

Chips and scratches are the most common types of auto body damage. If there is no dent in the metal, these are the easiest repairs for a do-it-yourselfer except when the scratches are very deep and very long. Find touch-up paint that matches your vehicle's colour at an auto supply centre.

How to Repair a Chip

1 Clean the area thoroughly with a wax and silicone remover.

2 Using a toothpick, slowly fill each chip with paint. You want to apply a series of thin layers rather than one large glob. Just touch the tip of the toothpick into the chip hole and allow the paint to naturally flow from the toothpick to the chip.

3 Move on to the next chip, leaving each application of paint to dry for at least 45 minutes.

4 Repeat the gradual application several times or until the crater is level with the surrounding surface.

5 If you have a clear-coat finish, the clear coat should be the last layer you add to reach a level surface.

6 After the paint is totally dry, use a tiny bit of polishing compound to make the repair blend in, followed by protective wax to protect your work.

How to Repair a Scratch

1 Clean the area thoroughly with a wax remover.

2 Scratches less than an inch long and shallow are best handled using the toothpick technique described for chip repairs.

3 Longer or deeper scratches require a brush, either the one supplied with the touch-up paint, or a fine artist's brush.

4 Apply the paint in thin layers, not one large glob. Use a tiny dab of paint on the brush, and apply it only inside the scratch, not on the surrounding paint.

5 Allow paint to dry thoroughly before applying the next layer.

6 Apply the final or clear-coat last layer as carefully as possible.

7 Often scratch repairs also require a bit of sanding to blend the repair. After the paint has dried for at least 48 hours, use the sanding block and first 1000-grit, then 1500-grit wet/dry sandpaper to lightly sand the repair. Use lots of water. You are simply trying to get the new paint level with the old.

Alternate Method: Apply Rubbing Compound & Protective Wax

Surface scratches can often be removed without using paint. Clean the area, then first use a non-silicone based polishing compound, followed by rubbing compound to see if the scratch can be erased. If there are numerous light surface scratches, using an electric buffer with the polishing compound is the quickest method. Complete the job with a coat of protective wax.

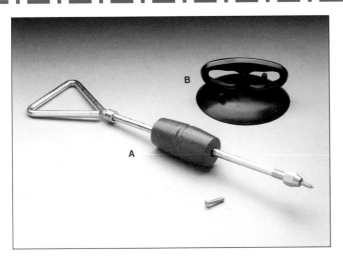

Slide-hammer dent puller (A), *suction-cup dent puller (B).*

Using a Dent Puller

If a dent is more than about ⅛" deep, you don't have much choice except to pull it out before applying body filler. Never try to fill a dent this deep with filler. The idea with pullers isn't to get the sheet metal perfectly back to its original shape, just approximately so, but never higher than original. Body filler is then used to finish the repair. Use the suction puller for large but shallow dents with soft edges; the slide-hammer for all others.

Using a Suction-cup Puller

❑ Use on fairly smooth, large dents where there's no creasing.

❑ Wet the dent with water, then press the suction cup into it. Push the air out of the cup and then pull slowly up and out. Be careful not to go too far.

❑ If there's no release button on the suction cup, slide it to one side until the seal is broken.

❑ Do not try to pull the dent out all at once. Move the suction cup around, pulling different portions of the dent, slowly working it out.

Using a Slide-hammer Puller

❑ Use on dents that are more than ⅛" deep that have sharp creases and edges. Try to determine the point of impact, usually the deepest part of the dent. Mark this spot.

❑ Using a marker, continue mapping out the dent, locating pulling points about an inch apart, working your way up to the undamaged sheet metal.

❑ Using a drill bit smaller than the metal screw in the puller, drill holes at the marks you made.

❑ Insert the puller screw into the hole at the deepest part of the dent, and after the screw gets started, turn it in about two full turns more.

❑ To pull out the dent, slide the weight quickly from the bottom to the top of the handle, hitting the handle solidly. Tap the handle a few times until the metal moves. Then move on to the next hole.

❑ Start in the deepest spot and work progressively around the dent. Take your time; you can't pull out the dent in one whack. You will often have to work four or five of the holes before you start to see results. Make a couple of passes around the dent, checking your progress with a straight-edge. You're done when no part of the dent is more than ⅛" below the surface.

❑ Always keep the puller at 90° to the surface. If it's at an angle, the sheet metal will be pulled in that direction.

Use a palm sander with 40-grit sandpaper to sand the repair area down to bare metal.

Repairing Basic Dents

Once a dent has been pulled out, or if it is no deeper than ⅛", you have to fill the area until it matches the surrounding sheet metal.

How to Repair a Basic Dent

1 Once the dent is pulled out, or if it is shallow enough (less than ⅛" deep) to not require pulling, sand the area with a palm sander equipped with 40-grit paper.

2 Sand the area around the dent and into the dent's centre (photo above). You have to get down to bare metal for the body filler to adhere.

3 Create a smooth transition from the paint to the bare metal by sanding the edges of the area with 180- to 220-grit paper. Get the transition area smooth to the touch.

4 Clean the area with a clean rag dampened with mineral spirits to remove any sanding residue.

5 Stir the filler thoroughly to an even colour and consistency (follow manufacturer's directions).

6 Place a small amount of filler on your plastic mixing board. A golf-ball-sized glob is enough for several small dents.

7 Squeeze the container of hardener repeatedly to mix it, then squeeze a small amount onto the filler. Blend the hardener and filler as you would cake batter, mixing them thoroughly over the course of only a minute or two. **NOTE:** It is better to start with too little hardener than too much. If you use too much, the filler will stiffen very quickly, becoming useless for application.

8 As soon as it is mixed, press the filler firmly into the dent with the applicator.

9 Apply thin coats until the repair area is slightly higher than the surrounding area.

10 After the filler has dried, begin sanding with a rubber sanding block and 80-grit paper, working from the outside edges to the centre.

11 Switch to 220-grit sandpaper as you get closer to the original paint surface. Clean the area between sandings.

12 If you have a low spot, repeat steps 6 through 11. Be patient and take your time.

13 Once the surface is smooth, outline it with masking tape, wipe it clean with a tack rag and spray on a coat of primer.

14 When dry, lightly sand the primer, feathering the edges.

15 Apply spot putty over the primer to fill any pinholes in the body filler that the primer may have revealed. Sand, apply primer and lightly sand again.

16 Spray successive thin coats of paint, building the colour up to match.

17 After the paint is dry and has had 30 days to cure, rub the area with a non-silicone based polishing compound to make the paint transition invisible, followed by a coat of protective wax.

Use the plastic body filler applicator to spread a series of thin coats of the filler on the repair area. Do not apply filler in thick coats; it will not dry and cure properly, and it may crack or contain large air bubbles.

Fixing Loose Exterior Trim

Loose body trim is annoying and makes your car look its worst. Fixing it is usually quite simple. You will need some adhesive remover and double-sided tape intended for body trim from your auto centre.

Don't glue the loose section of trim or moulding back on. You will probably make a repair that won't last very long. Instead, carefully peel the loose trim all the way off. You may need to use adhesive remover to do so. Using adhesive remover, carefully clean off all traces of the old adhesive from the back of the trim. Then clean the body panel where the trim was, being careful not to damage the paint.

Use some masking tape to create two strips along the body panel, to serve as a guide for positioning the trim. Attach the double-sided mounting tape to the back of the trim. For wide pieces of trim, you may need to use two strips of tape. Before peeling away the backing paper, hold the trim up to the body panel and make sure a single layer of tape is thick enough to line up the trim with other pieces. If not, use a double thickness to make up the difference.

Peel off the backing paper of the mounting tape, and position the trim. Start at one end and work your way down the length of the trim, pressing it firmly into place.

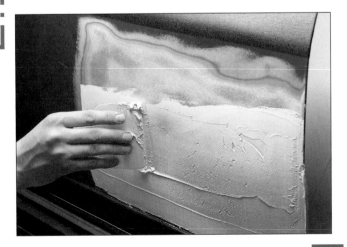

Wiring a Trailer Connection

There are three keys to trouble-free trailer wiring: (1) a solid ground, (2) wiring connections that won't work loose, (3) weatherproofed wiring. Also check these elements when your trailer lights won't work. Repairing or installing trouble-free trailer wiring is a great do-it-yourself project. Not only will you have a better installation than you could get otherwise, but you will be prepared to deal with any problems down the road. Here are some helpful ideas:

❏ If you're having problems with existing trailer wiring, check the ground connections first. Establishing a solid electrical ground isn't hard, but many people tend to treat it as unimportant. The trailer's electrical connection should have a ground wire ending in a ring terminal bolted firmly to an unpainted metal portion of the trailer. If it doesn't, add one (see next page). Don't rely on the trailer ball for an electrical ground, because it won't be adequate.

❏ Good wiring connections are those with the fewest splices possible. Anytime there is a splice, make it permanent, using crimped, plastic-covered connectors sealed with heat shrink tubing.

❏ To weatherproof connectors when not in use, buy another inexpensive connector kit with larger male and female connectors. Fill them with dielectric grease available at auto centres, and use them as protective caps.

RECOMMENDED POWER TOOLS

MASTERCRAFT

DRILL

• heat gun

RECOMMENDED HAND TOOLS

• combination wire tool

NEEDED MATERIALS

• waterproof crimp connectors
• shrink tubing
• wire

Use a heat gun to make the shrink tubing mould properly around the connection.

❑ For new installations, purchase complete trailer wiring kits, rather than make your own wiring harnesses. You will get good instructions and all the necessary hardware for a quick, trouble-free installation.

❑ When selecting a location for the ground wire, thoroughly remove dirt and rust-proofing material down to bare metal from an area on the trailer or vehicle frame. Drill a hole and install a self-tapping screw through the ground wire ring terminal.

❑ When making a new installation, first twist all wire connections together and perform a circuit test. Step on the brake pedal, and start the turn signal flashers and parking lights to be certain your wiring work is correct. If everything checks out, make permanent connections as detailed below.

How to Make Trailer Wiring Connections

1 Cut a 2" piece of shrink tubing and slide it onto one of the wires far enough to be out of the way.

2 Crimp both wires into the waterproof connector, then slide the tubing over the connector.

3 Use a heat gun to shrink the tubing until it moulds around the connection. Do not let it melt. **NOTE:** It may be necessary to install a heavy-duty flasher to eliminate signal flashing that is too rapid or slow.

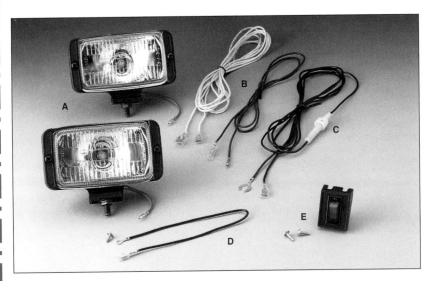

A typical driving or fog lamp kit contains: *lamps (A), wiring harnesses for the lamps (B), a power supply wire containing a fuse (C), a ground wire (D), and a switch (E).*

Installing Driving & Fog Lamps

Auxiliary driving and fog lamps illuminate more of the road than regular headlights, greatly increasing visibility at night or in poor weather conditions. Driving lights provide a longer beam spread – up to 1.2 km (¾ mi) – than regular headlights. They let you see much farther ahead and react more quickly to conditions. Fog lights throw a wider but lower beam that keeps foul weather from blinding you. Both types of lights are easy to install.

Invest the extra few dollars to purchase a complete lamp kit. It will give you a pre-assembled wire harness that includes a relay, two in-line fuses and a three-terminal switch. If you purchase items separately, you will have to figure out everything you need on your own.

RECOMMENDED POWER TOOLS

MASTERCRAFT

DRILL

RECOMMENDED HAND TOOLS

MASTERCRAFT

BASIC HAND TOOLS

- centre punch
- file

NEEDED MATERIALS

- silcone caulk
- plastic ties
- shrink tubing

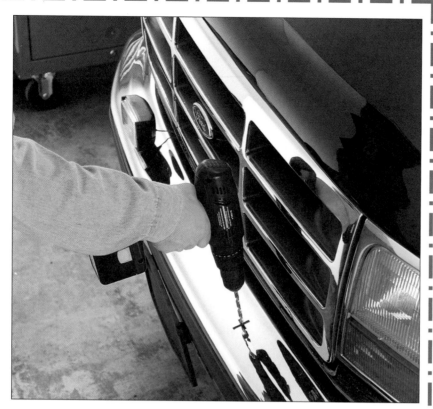

Drill holes for mounting the lamps. *You may need to use a centre punch when drilling holes on a metal bumper to keep the drill bit in position when starting the hole.*

How to Install Driving & Fog Lamps

1 Decide where you want to locate the lamps. They can be mounted on either the top or bottom of the bumper. Check local regulations; there are often limits on mounting heights. These usually are 12" to 30" from the ground for fog lamps and 16" to 42" for driving lamps.

2 Disconnect the negative battery cable. If you have a battery memory keeper (see Tip, page 23), use it.

3 Determine locations for mounting the lamps. Be sure not to obstruct headlights or turn signals. **NOTE:** Vehicles equipped with airbags often have sensors located inside the front bumpers. Check your owner's manual or with your dealer to determine their location before drilling any holes.

TIP:
Check local regulations regarding the number of lights that can be turned on at one time – most municipalities do not allow high beams and auxiliary driving lamps to be on at the same time.

Find an existing location *where wires pass through the firewall (A) and use this spot to route the lamp kit wires to the switch.*

4 Drill holes for mounting the lamps at the locations you determined. Follow manufacturer's instructions for the size hole you need to create. Use a file to remove any rough edges around the hole.

5 Coat each lamp's mounting bolt with silicone caulk (to prevent rusting) and insert them through the holes. Use the lock washers and nuts to attach them to the bumper. Follow manufacturer's instructions when mounting the lamps; some lamps will require reversing the position of the lens and reflector within the lamp units if they are mounted on the bottom of the bumper.

6 Locate and install the switch within easy reach of the driver. Under the dash or on the console is best. Drill holes using the mounting bracket as a guide. Be careful – make sure there is 1" clearance behind the mounting area on the dash or console.

7 Following all manufacturer's instructions and safety warnings, carefully run and connect the wires from the lamps to the switch, and from the switch to the power supply. The power supply will be either the positive terminal on the battery or the vehicle's fuse box, whichever is most convenient (this will usually be the fuse box since it is often in the dash area). Try to avoid drilling any holes through the firewall. Instead, find an existing wire or cable and run the new wires through this opening.

8 Where possible, use shrink tubing to weatherproof connections in the engine compartment. (See pages 52 – 53 for directions on using shrink tubing.)

9 Install the in-line fuse in the power supply wire and reconnect the battery's negative cable.

10 Test and troubleshoot your new lighting system (the manufacturer's instructions will have information to help you figure out any problems with the system). Once you're sure the lights work properly, secure all wires neatly. Plastic ties work best for this. Make sure the wiring is clear of hot or moving parts.

__Locate the switch__ in a spot where it is easy to reach but will not interfere with other accessories or switches.

11 Slightly loosen the mounting nut on each lamp. Aim the lamps according to the manufacturer's instructions. If no aiming information is provided, follow these guidelines: With the vehicle parked on a level surface about 25' from a wall, measure the distance from the ground to the centre of the new lamps. Next, measure from the centre of the vehicle front to the centre of each lamp. Transfer these lines to the wall with chalk. Adjust the light beam so it is 1½" below the horizontal centre line, and 15" from the centre line of the vehicle.

12 Tighten the mounting nuts on the driving and fog lamps.

TROUBLESHOOTING

Your ears often provide the first warning of car trouble. Here is how to recognize the problem behind what you hear:

FROM THE SUSPENSION:

You Hear: Clunks, pops and rattles in response to road bumps.
Problem: Could be suspension and steering components, or loose exhaust system parts.

You Hear: Grinding or growling sound noticeable when turning.
Problem: The wheel bearings are the most likely cause.

You Hear: Rhythmical metallic click while driving.
Problem: Loose hubcap or wheel bearing.

FROM THE BRAKES:

You Hear: Light squeaking on light to medium brake applications.
Problem: Relatively normal characteristic of disc brakes. If heard when brakes are not in use, the brake wear indicators are in need of service.

You Hear: An occasional heavy grinding or groaning.
Problem: Can be normal, or can be brake dust trapped in the pads.

You Hear: High-pitched squeaking whenever brakes are applied.
Problem: Loose brake pad, or glazed pads or rotor/drum.

You Hear: Chattering as brakes are applied.
Problem: Contaminated or broken brake pads, or brake rotors and drums that are warped.

FROM THE EXHAUST:

You Hear: Sudden increase in exhaust noise volume or tone.
Problem: Failed muffler or a hole somewhere in the exhaust system. The louder the sound, the farther forward the damage.

FROM THE ENGINE:

You Hear: Squealing.
Problem: Loose or worn drive belt.

You Hear: Continuous hum or whine that may get louder at times.
Problem: The alternator or water pump, or if the whine gets louder as you turn the steering wheel, the power-steering pump.

You Hear: Deep rhythmical thumping or thudding.
Problem: The engine's main or rod bearings are the likely suspects.

You Hear: Soft, rhythmical slapping that may stop as the engine warms up.
Problem: Called "piston slap," it is okay as long as it goes away once the engine is warm. Otherwise have it checked by a professional.

You Hear: Irregular snapping or clicking, along with a rough-running engine or a loss of power.
Problem: Electrical arcing in the distributor cap or spark plugs.

You Hear: Pinging.
Problem: Engine out of tune; also make sure you are using grade of gasoline recommended in owner's manual.

FROM THE TRANSMISSION OR DRIVETRAIN:

You Hear: Whine or howl, most evident in Park or Neutral.
Problem: A damaged hydraulic pump in the transmission or the torque converter.

You Hear: Progressively louder clicking as the steering wheel in a front wheel drive vehicle is turned.
Problem: Faulty constant velocity (CV) joint, (it allows the drive axle to rotate at various angles).

You Hear: Resonant howl or whine only when accelerating or decelerating.
Problem: Dry or damaged differential gears and bearings.

Troubleshooting a Non-starting Engine

Depending on whether it is a "cranking no-start" (your engine turns over but does not start) or a "no-crank condition" (you turn the key and only hear silence) you may be able to get the engine started.

CRANKING NO-START

All Engines

❑ Make sure the vehicle has gas.

❑ Check to see if the air filter is clogged with leaves or debris.

❑ Check for spark. Remove a spark plug wire and insert the tip of a screwdriver into the plug cable. Place the screwdriver shaft about ¼" from a good ground, away from any gasoline (photo below). **NOTE:** Do not touch the screwdriver while cranking the engine to prevent shock. See if there is a blue or white spark jumping between the screwdriver and the ground when you crank the engine. If you see a spark, the problem is most likely in the fuel system. Check the fuel pump fuse. If you do not

Check to see if electricity is flowing to the spark plugs when your vehicle's starter will crank but the engine will not start. Test for a spark at the end of the spark plug cable using a screwdriver placed in the end of the cable (see method above).

see any spark, you will need to get a tow to the repair shop.

❑ Check the fuses if the "Check Engine" or "Service Engine Soon" light does not come on with the key in the "On" position.

❑ With the key "Off," carefully disconnect one wire connector at a time from around the distributor cap, coil packs and fuel injectors. Remove any corrosion, reattach and try again.

❑ Clean the spark plugs or install a new set. This usually is neither difficult nor expensive.

Fuel Injected Engines

❑ "Prime" the fuel system by turning the key to the "On" or "Run" position for 10 seconds, then off for 30 seconds, then to the "Start" position.

❑ Hold the accelerator all the way down to the floor while cranking. This shuts the fuel "Off" and will help clear a flooded engine.

Carbureted Engines

❑ With the air cleaner removed, hold down the accelerator and check for gasoline spray inside the carburetor. If there is no spray, try pouring an ounce or two of gas down the carburetor to prime the fuel system. If this gets you going, you need a new fuel pump.

NO-CRANK CONDITION

❑ Clean and tighten the battery cable connections. Even if they look okay, there could be corrosion you cannot see. Remember to always disconnect the negative cable first and reconnect the negative last.

❑ Try giving the battery a jump start from a helper car (see page 26).

- A bad neutral safety switch could make you think the battery is dead. Place the shift selector of an automatic transmission in Neutral, set the parking brake, place your foot firmly on the brake pedal and try restarting. If the engine starts, have your repair shop test the switch before installing a new one.

- Manual transmissions have a clutch safety switch. Make sure the carpet or floor mat is not keeping the pedal from going all the way down.

- Disconnect, disable or by-pass any security or alarm systems. This will eliminate these items as causes of the problem.

- Check the cables that run from the battery to the engine block and starter motor for fraying, corrosion or looseness. Clean all connections, plus firmly tighten all attaching fasteners.

- Are the battery cables warm? A defective starter drawing excess current could be the cause. Let the starter cool down, then try a jump start. Whether the engine starts or not, you will need a new starter motor.

- If all else fails, it is time to call the local towing service for a trip to the repair shop.

TROUBLESHOOTING HOT & COLD WEATHER DRIVEABILITY PROBLEMS

Hot and cold weather starting and driveability problems have been common since the first internal combustion engine was turned over. Although many advances, in both engine design and gasoline, have been made over the years, problems still exist in both fuel injection and carbureted fuel systems. Check the following if you are experiencing either hot or cold driveability problems:

General Problems

- The problem may be as simple as the gas you are using. Switch to a different brand for a couple of tankfuls and see if there is any improvement.

- Check the air filter. Make sure it is not dirty and seals tightly inside the air filter housing. A leaking air filter housing will cause a vacuum leak.

- Be certain you have the correct PCV valve. Only use the same manufacturer and part number as the original valve. The wrong one (even though it may look and fit the same as the PCV valve you just removed) or a dirty valve can produce numerous driveability problems.

- A partially clogged fuel filter can cause hard starting, bucking and stalling. Replace it.

- Check for leaking, pinched or collapsed vacuum hoses (the small soft rubber tubes on top of the engine). Many emission control devices and sensors that affect driveability are vacuum operated. Repair or replace these hoses as necessary.

- Check for leaking, pinched or collapsed fuel line hoses, especially under the hood. Excess engine heat can weaken the inner walls of rubber fuel line hoses, especially where a hose may have to make a sharp bend around an obstacle. Replace the hoses if they feel soft or mushy.

Some troubleshooting will be much easier if you have a helper operate inside the vehicle while you look under the hood.

Cold-weather Starting Problems with Fuel Injected Engines

❑ Check for a weak battery. When buying a replacement, always purchase one with as much cold cranking capacity as possible.

❑ Check for carbon build-up on the throttle plate inside the carburetor. Even a small amount of carbon will absorb gasoline vapours, preventing the gas from burning correctly. Use a special fuel injector, throttle body and air intake cleaning kit to remove the excess carbon, gum and varnish.

❑ Look inside the air cleaner housing. Debris entangled in the sensors will cause improper readings. Carefully remove any leaves and dirt from the emission sensors located inside the air cleaner housing.

Cold-weather Starting Problems with Carbureted Engines

❑ Check for weak battery. When buying a replacement, always purchase one with as much cold cranking capacity as possible.

❑ Be certain you are "setting" the choke (closing the choke plate which is at the top of the carburetor) by depressing the accelerator once before turning the ignition. The choke plate should slam shut. If the choke linkage is dirty, it will bind and the choke will stay open. Spray the linkage with gum cutter to remove any built-up varnish, then lubricate the linkage with spray lubricant to prevent the problem from reoccuring.

❑ Watch the choke linkage and throttle plate while cranking the engine. The choke vacuum break should open the choke plate slightly. If the choke does not open, the rubber diaphragm inside the vacuum break is defective and will need to be replaced.

❑ Check to see if the flexible pre-heat tube from the exhaust manifold to the air cleaner is missing. The hot air drawn off the engine helps gasoline burn easier. Replace if missing, cut or damaged.

❑ Look inside the air cleaner intake. A failed or stuck thematic air cleaner vacuum motor or heat sensor can keep the dampener valve inside the air cleaner from closing. If you notice any problems with the choke system, it is best to have your repair shop handle the repairs.

Hot-weather Driveability Problems on Fuel Injected & Carbureted Vehicles

❑ Be certain you have the correct gas cap for your vehicle. The wrong cap will cause poor driveability due to too high fuel pressure, vapour lock and overheated fuel. If in doubt, replace the cap.

❏ Do not top off the fuel tank on hot days. The gasoline will expand, cause vapour lock and a rough, unsteady idle.

❏ Check the charcoal canister filter. If it is saturated with gasoline, the air/fuel mixture will have too much fuel and the engine will stall. Replace the canister and filter with a new one. Check your owner's manual for location.

❏ An overheating engine will cause poor fuel economy, lack of power and engine pinging. Check the fan belts and adjust if necessary. Check the coolant level and level of protection. Be sure the coolant system is using a 50/50 mix of antifreeze and water.

❏ A stuck or mis-calibrated coolant system thermostat will cause poor fuel economy and higher than normal tailpipe emissions. If your engine is taking too long to reach operating temperature (about 5 minutes under normal conditions), or when you test the heater it doesn't create enough hot air, replace the thermostat.

❏ A malfunctioning high-speed fan, of a two-speed electric coolant fan, will cause the engine to run hotter than usual. With the hood closed, wait until the coolant fan turns on. Then flip on the air conditioning. The high-speed fan should come on. If it does not, have your repair shop find out why.

If you need to tow your vehicle, make sure the tow strap is hooked to a part of the vehicle that will withstand the stress. Some vehicles have towing loops welded to the frame for such a purpose.

Emergency Situations

Keeping your vehicle in good shape is the best way to prevent breakdowns. But still, you may find yourself in such a situation. Here are a few ideas to make the experience go as smoothly as possible.

Handling Emergency Situations

❏ Usually your vehicle will give you some warnings that it is about to stop. When you sense this, try to steer over to the right-hand shoulder of the road and as far off the driving lanes as possible. Even if you have a tire blow out, first make certain you have control of the vehicle and then move to the right shoulder. If your vehicle does stop dead in the middle of a busy street or highway, stay inside. Wait for police to control traffic before risking moving around the vehicle or trying to cross the road.

❏ If you have a breakdown that you are not prepared for, staying in your vehicle is usually the best thing to do. This is particularly true in bad weather, especially in winter. Walking along or attempting to cross busy roads is very dangerous. Wait for help to arrive – it will.

❏ Set out flares from your emergency kit if your breakdown is at night. Place them about 15' behind your car to notify traffic there is a problem ahead.

❏ If the engine still runs, do not run it continually – even if it is very cold. Group all of the passengers together to conserve body heat. Use the blanket and candle from your emergency kit (see page 47). Turn on the engine occasionally for warmth, but never run an engine while stationary without lowering a window slightly so there is no danger of carbon monoxide poisoning.

❏ Never attempt to tow a vehicle unless the transmission can be placed in neutral and

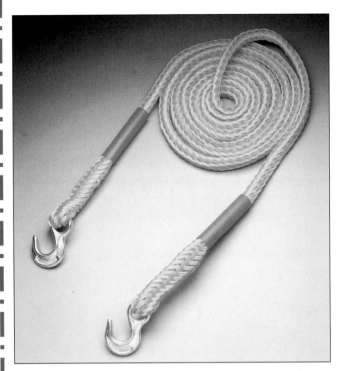

If you must tow your vehicle, *make sure you have a towing strap rated to handle your vehicle's weight. Also, wait until the roads have less traffic on them before attempting to move your vehicle.*

all of the wheels turn freely, or you can raise the drive wheels off the ground. Towing a vehicle with a locked-up transmission will cause serious damage to the transmission.

❏ When towing, it is best if you can stay at 40 km/hr (25 mph) or lower and travel the shortest distance possible to get your vehicle to a place where it can be repaired.

❏ Find a strong frame member or bracket to which you can attach the tow strap (photo opposite page). A bumper is not secure enough to handle the stress. Do not attach anything to moving parts, like struts or torsion bars, or around hoses. If you are not certain of a spot to attach the tow strap, wait for assistance. It is very dangerous to tow a vehicle that is not properly secured.

Index

A

Air cleaner, 12, 57
Air filter, 12, 58
   replacement schedule, 17
Air/fuel mixture, adjusting, 14
Alignment, 18, 36, 40-42
All-wheel drive
   tire rotation schedule, 18
Alternator, 13, 56
   checking & adjusting belt, 32
Antifreeze/coolant, 34
   leaks, 33
   mixing with water, 46, 60
Automatic transmission, 14
   maintenance schedule, 17-19
   service, 18, 19

B

Battery, 22
   checking & cleaning, 23, 46, 58
   disconnecting, 20, 22, 57
   jump-starting a vehicle, 26, 27
   leaking battery, 33
Belt-driven camshaft engine, 18
Belts
   adjusting & replacing, 32
   checking, 46
Body filler, 49-51
Body trim, repairing loose, 51
Brake booster, 13
Brake system & brakes, 13, 15
   components of brake system, 15
   leaking fluid, 33
   maintenance schedule, 17
   pads, 39, 56
   troubleshooting, 18, 38, 39, 56
   using parking brake, 38
   wheel cylinder, 15
Bumpy ride, causes, 36, 56

C

Cam sensor, 13
Carbureted engines, 13, 57-59
Catalytic converter, 15
Charcoal canister filter, 17
Chip in paint, repairing, 48

Choke, setting, 59
City driving, 18, 19
Clicking sound, causes, 56
Cooling system, 13, 14, 60
   coolant composition, 34
   fluid leaks, 33
   flush & fill, 17, 46
   mixing coolant with water, 46
   radiator, 14, 34, 45
Crank sensor, 13
CV (constant velocity) joint, 56
Cylinder block, 13
Cylinder head, 13

D

Dent, repairing, 49-51
Diesel fuel leak, 33
Differential, 14, 15, 56
Disc brake caliper, 15
Distributor & cap, 13, 24, 25, 56
Dog-tracking, 39
Door locks, lubricating in cold
   weather, 47
Drive axle, 14
Drive belt, 14
   adjusting & replacing, 32
   checking, 46, 56
Driving lamps, installing, 53-55

E

ECM, see: ECU
ECU (electronic control unit), 14
EGR (exhaust gas recirculation)
   valve & filter, 17
Electrical system
   battery, 20, 22, 23, 33, 46
   cleaning connections, 20, 21
   distributor cap, 15, 24, 25
   rotor, 24, 25
   spark plugs & cables, 24, 25
   troubleshooting, 20, 21
   wiring trailer connection, 52, 53
Elevating & supporting vehicle, 8
Emergency situations, 61
Emission system, 60
Engine, diagrams of parts, 12-15
Exhaust system, 13, 14
   EGR valve & filter, 17
   muffler & repairs, 15, 44

   troubleshooting, 56
   venting exhaust while
     working, 9

F

Firewall, 14
Fogging windshield, reducing, 46
Fog lamps, installing, 53-55
Four-wheel drive, tire rotation, 18
Front wheel drive
   suspension system, 36
   tire rotation schedule, 18
   transaxle, 14
   troubleshooting noises, 56
Fuel economy, increasing, 18, 24
Fuel filter, 17, 58
Fuel injection system, 13, 14, 57-59
Fuel injector, 14
Fuel pressure regulator, 14
Fuses, blown, 20, 57

G

Gasket, replacing or reusing, 16
Gasoline, 60
   grades & types, 34, 58
   leak, 33
Gloves for working, 9
Grease drips, 33
Grinding sound, causes, 56

H

Headlights, replacing, 28, 29
Heater hoses, 14
Howling sound, causes, 56
Hydrometer to check battery, 23

I

IAC (idle air control), 14
Idle speed, regulating, 14
Ignition coil, 13
Intake manifold, 14
Intake valve, 13

J

Jack, proper use, 8, 43
Jack stand, 8, 42, 44
Jumper cables, 26, 47
Jump-starting a vehicle, 26, 27

L

Leaks, identifying & fixing, 33

M

Maintenance schedules, 16, 17
Manifold, see: Intake manifold
Manual transmission, 17-19, 58
Master cylinder, 14